Grundgesetz der Bundesrep.....

Basic Law for the Federal Republic of Germany

German constitution

www.highcontentbooks.com

1st. Edition 2021

Translated by: Professor Christian Tomuschat, Professor David P. Currie, Professor Donald P. Kommers and Raymond Kerr, in cooperation with the Language Service of the German Bundestag

Version information: The translation includes the amendment(s) to the Act by Article 1 of the Act of 28 March 2019 (Federal Law Gazette I p. 404)

For conditions governing use of this translation, please see the information provided at www.gesetze-im-internet.de under "Translations".

Basic Law for the Federal Republic of Germany

Basic Law for the Federal Republic of Germany in the revised version published in the Federal Law Gazette Part III, classification number 100-1, as last amended by Article 1 of the Act of 28 March 2019 (Federal Law Gazette I p. 404).

The Parliamentary Council, meeting in public session at Bonn am Rhein on 23 May 1949, confirmed that the Basic Law for the Federal Republic of Germany, which was adopted by the Parliamentary Council on 8 May 1949, was ratified in the week of 16 to 22 May 1949 by the parliaments of more than two thirds of the participating German *Länder.*

By virtue of this fact the Parliamentary Council, represented by its Presidents, has signed and promulgated the Basic Law.

The Basic Law is hereby published in the Federal Law Gazette pursuant to paragraph (3) of Article 145.

Content

Preamble

Conscious of their responsibility before God and man,

Inspired by the determination to promote world peace as an equal partner in a united Europe, the German people, in the exercise of their constituent power, have adopted this Basic Law.

Germans in the *Länder* of Baden-Württemberg, Bavaria, Berlin, Brandenburg, Bremen, Hamburg, Hesse, Lower Saxony, Mecklenburg-Western Pomerania, North Rhine-Westphalia, Rhineland-Palatinate, Saarland, Saxony, Saxony-Anhalt, Schleswig-Holstein and Thuringia have achieved the unity and freedom of Germany in free self-determination. This Basic Law thus applies to the entire German people.

I. Basic Rights

Article 1 [Human dignity – Human rights – Legally binding force of basic rights]

(1) Human dignity shall be inviolable. To respect and protect it shall be the duty of all state authority.

(2) The German people therefore acknowledge inviolable and inalienable human rights as the basis of every community, of peace and of justice in the world.

(3) The following basic rights shall bind the legislature, the executive and the judiciary as directly applicable law.

Article 2 [Personal freedoms]

(1) Every person shall have the right to free development of his personality insofar as he does not violate the rights of others or offend against the constitutional order or the moral law.

(2) Every person shall have the right to life and physical integrity. Freedom of the person shall be inviolable. These rights may be interfered with only pursuant to a law.

Article 3 [Equality before the law]
(1) All persons shall be equal before the law.

(2) Men and women shall have equal rights. The state shall promote the actual implementation of equal rights for women and men and take steps to eliminate disadvantages that now exist.

(3) No person shall be favoured or disfavoured because of sex, parentage, race, language, homeland and origin, faith or religious or political opinions. No person shall be disfavoured because of disability.

Article 4 [Freedom of faith and conscience]
(1) Freedom of faith and of conscience and freedom to profess a religious or philosophical creed shall be inviolable.

(2) The undisturbed practice of religion shall be guaranteed.

(3) No person shall be compelled against his conscience to render military service involving the use of arms. Details shall be regulated by a federal law.

Article 5 [Freedom of expression, arts and sciences]
(1) Every person shall have the right freely to express and disseminate his opinions in speech, writing and pictures and to inform himself without hindrance from generally accessible sources. Freedom of the press and freedom of reporting by means of broadcasts and films shall be guaranteed. There shall be no censorship.

(2) These rights shall find their limits in the provisions of general laws, in provisions for the protection of young persons and in the right to personal honour.

(3) Arts and sciences, research and teaching shall be free. The freedom of teaching shall not release any person from allegiance to the constitution.

Article 6 [Marriage – Family – Children]

(1) Marriage and the family shall enjoy the special protection of the state.

(2) The care and upbringing of children is the natural right of parents and a duty primarily incumbent upon them. The state shall watch over them in the performance of this duty.

(3) Children may be separated from their families against the will of their parents or guardians only pursuant to a law and only if the parents or guardians fail in their duties or the children are otherwise in danger of serious neglect.

(4) Every mother shall be entitled to the protection and care of the community.

(5) Children born outside of marriage shall be provided by legislation with the same opportunities for physical and mental development and for their position in society as are enjoyed by those born within marriage.

Article 7 [School system]

(1) The entire school system shall be under the supervision of the state.

(2) Parents and guardians shall have the right to decide whether children shall receive religious instruction.

(3) Religious instruction shall form part of the regular curriculum in state schools, with the exception of non-denominational schools. Without prejudice to the state's right of supervision, religious instruction shall be given in accordance with the tenets of the religious community concerned. Teachers may not be obliged against their will to give religious instruction.

(4) The right to establish private schools shall be guaranteed. Private schools that serve as alternatives to state schools shall require the approval of the state and shall be subject to the laws of the *Länder*. Such approval shall be given when private schools are not inferior to the state schools in terms of their educational aims, their facilities or the professional training of their teaching staff and when segregation of pupils according to the means of their parents will not be encouraged thereby. Approval shall be withheld if the economic and legal position of the teaching staff is not adequately assured.

(5) A private elementary school shall be approved only if the education authority finds that it serves a special educational interest or if, on the application of parents or guardians, it is to be established as a denominational or interdenominational school or as a school based on a particular philosophy and no state elementary school of that type exists in the municipality.

(6) Preparatory schools shall remain abolished.

Article 8 [Freedom of assembly]

(1) All Germans shall have the right to assemble peacefully and unarmed without prior notification or permission.

(2) In the case of outdoor assemblies, this right may be restricted by or pursuant to a law.

Article 9 [Freedom of association]

(1) All Germans shall have the right to form societies and other associations.

(2) Associations whose aims or activities contravene the criminal laws or that are directed against the constitutional order or the concept of international understanding shall be prohibited.

(3) The right to form associations to safeguard and improve working and economic conditions shall be guaranteed to every individual and to every occupation or profession. Agreements that restrict or seek to impair this right shall be null and void; measures directed to this end shall be unlawful. Measures taken pursuant to Article 12a, to paragraphs (2) and (3) of Article 35, to paragraph (4) of Article 87a or to Article 91 may not be directed against industrial disputes engaged in by associations within the meaning of the first sentence of this paragraph in order to safeguard and improve working and economic conditions.

Article 10 [Privacy of correspondence, posts and telecommunications]

(1) The privacy of correspondence, posts and telecommunications shall be inviolable.

(2) Restrictions may be ordered only pursuant to a law. If the restriction serves to protect the free democratic basic order or the existence or security of the Federation or of a *Land*, the law may provide that the person affected shall not be informed of the restriction and that recourse to the courts shall be replaced by a review of the case by agencies and auxiliary agencies appointed by the legislature.

Article 11 [Freedom of movement]

(1) All Germans shall have the right to move freely throughout the federal territory.

(2) This right may be restricted only by or pursuant to a law, and only in cases in which the absence of adequate means of support would result in a particular burden for the community, or in which such restriction is necessary to avert an imminent danger to the existence or the free democratic basic order of the Federation or of a *Land*, to combat the danger of an epidemic, to respond to a grave accident or natural disaster, to protect young persons from serious neglect or to prevent crime.

Article 12 [Occupational freedom]

(1) All Germans shall have the right freely to choose their occupation or profession, their place of work and their place of training. The practice of an occupation or profession may be regulated by or pursuant to a law.

(2) No person may be required to perform work of a particular kind except within the framework of a traditional duty of community service that applies generally and equally to all.

(3) Forced labour may be imposed only on persons deprived of their liberty by the judgment of a court.

Article 12a [Compulsory military and alternative civilian service]

(1) Men who have attained the age of eighteen may be required to serve in the Armed Forces, in the Federal Border Police, or in a civil defence organisation.

(2) Any person who, on grounds of conscience, refuses to render military service involving the use of arms may be required to perform alternative service. The duration of alternative service shall not exceed that of military service. Details shall be regulated by a law, which shall not interfere with the freedom to make a decision in accordance with the dictates of conscience and which shall also provide for the possibility of alternative service not connected with units of the Armed Forces or of the Federal Border Police.

(3) Persons liable to compulsory military service who are not called upon to render service pursuant to paragraph (1) or (2) of this Article may, when a state of defence is in effect, be assigned by or pursuant to a law to employment involving civilian services for defence purposes, including the protection of the civilian population; they may be assigned to public employment only for the purpose of discharging police functions or such other sovereign functions of public administration as can be discharged only by persons employed in the public service. The employment contemplated by the first sentence of this paragraph may include services within the Armed Forces, in the provision of military supplies or with public administrative authorities; assignments to employment connected with supplying and servicing the civilian population shall be permissible only to meet their basic requirements or to guarantee their safety.

(4) If, during a state of defence, the need for civilian services in the civilian health system or in stationary military hospitals cannot be met on a voluntary basis, women between the age of eighteen and fifty-five may be called upon to render such services by or pursuant to a law. Under no circumstances may they be required to render service involving the use of arms.

(5) Prior to the existence of a state of defence, assignments under paragraph (3) of this Article may be made only if the requirements of paragraph (1) of Article 80a are met. In preparation for the provision of services under paragraph (3) of this Article that demand special knowledge or skills, participation in training courses may be required by or pursuant to a law. In this case the first sentence of this paragraph shall not apply.

(6) If, during a state of defence, the need for workers in the areas specified in the second sentence of paragraph (3) of this Article cannot be met on a voluntary basis, the right of German citizens to abandon their occupation or place of employment may be restricted by or pursuant to a law in order to meet this need. Prior to the existence of a state of defence, the first sentence of paragraph (5) of this Article shall apply, *mutatis mutandis.*

Article 13 [Inviolability of the home]

(1) The home is inviolable.

(2) Searches may be authorised only by a judge or, when time is of the essence, by other authorities designated by the laws and may be carried out only in the manner therein prescribed.

(3) If particular facts justify the suspicion that any person has committed an especially serious crime specifically defined by a law, technical means of acoustical surveillance of any home in which the suspect is supposedly staying may be employed pursuant to judicial order for the purpose of prosecuting the offence, provided that alternative methods of investigating the matter would be disproportionately difficult or unproductive. The authorisation shall be for a limited time. The order shall be issued by a panel composed of three judges. When time is of the essence, it may also be issued by a single judge.

(4) To avert acute dangers to public safety, especially dangers to life or to the public, technical means of surveillance of the home may be employed only pursuant to judicial order. When time is of the essence, such measures may also be ordered by other authorities designated by a law; a judicial decision shall subsequently be obtained without delay.

(5) If technical means are contemplated solely for the protection of persons officially deployed in a home, the measure may be ordered by an authority designated by a law. The information thereby obtained may be otherwise used only for purposes of criminal prosecution or to avert danger and only if the legality of the measure has been previously determined by a judge; when time is of the essence, a judicial decision shall subsequently be obtained without delay.

(6) The Federal Government shall report to the Bundestag annually as to the employment of technical means pursuant to paragraph (3) and, within the jurisdiction of the Federation, pursuant to paragraph (4) and, insofar as judicial approval is required, pursuant to paragraph (5) of this Article. A panel elected by the Bundestag shall exercise parliamentary oversight on the basis of this report. A comparable parliamentary oversight shall be afforded by the *Länder*.

(7) Interferences and restrictions shall otherwise only be permissible to avert a danger to the public or to the life of an individual or, pursuant to a law, to confront an acute danger to public safety and order, in particular to relieve an accommodation shortage, to combat the danger of an epidemic or to protect young persons at risk.

Article 14 [Property – Inheritance – Expropriation]

(1) Property and the right of inheritance shall be guaranteed. Their content and limits shall be defined by the laws.

(2) Property entails obligations. Its use shall also serve the public good.

(3) Expropriation shall only be permissible for the public good. It may only be ordered by or pursuant to a law that determines the nature and extent of compensation. Such compensation shall be determined by establishing an equitable balance between the public interest and the interests of those affected.

In case of dispute concerning the amount of compensation, recourse may be had to the ordinary courts.

Article 15 [Nationalisation]

Land, natural resources and means of production may, for the purpose of nationalisation, be transferred to public ownership or other forms of public enterprise by a law that determines the nature and extent of compensation. With respect to such compensation the third and fourth sentences of paragraph (3) of Article 14 shall apply, *mutatis mutandis*.

Article 16 [Citizenship – Extradition]

(1) No German may be deprived of his citizenship. Loss of citizenship may occur only pursuant to a law and, if it occurs against the will of the person affected, only if he does not become stateless as a result.

(2) No German may be extradited to a foreign country. The law may provide otherwise for extraditions to a member state of the European Union or to an international court, provided that the rule of law is observed.

Article 16a [Right of asylum]

(1) Persons persecuted on political grounds shall have the right of asylum.

(2) Paragraph (1) of this Article may not be invoked by a person who enters the federal territory from a member state of the European Communities or from another third state in which application of the Convention Relating to the Status of Refugees and of the Convention for the Protection of Human Rights and Fundamental Freedoms is assured. The states outside the European Communities to which the conditions referred to in the first sentence of this paragraph apply shall be specified by a law requiring the consent of the Bundesrat. In the cases specified in the first sentence of this paragraph, measures to terminate an applicant's stay may be implemented without regard to any legal challenge that may have been instituted against them.

(3) By a law requiring the consent of the Bundesrat, states may be specified in which, on the basis of their laws, enforcement practices and general political conditions, it can be safely concluded that neither political persecution nor inhuman or degrading punishment or treatment exists. It shall be presumed that a foreigner from such a state is not persecuted, unless he presents evidence justifying the conclusion that, contrary to this presumption, he is persecuted on political grounds.

(4) In the cases specified by paragraph (3) of this Article and in other cases that are plainly unfounded or considered to be plainly unfounded, the implementation of measures to terminate an applicant's stay may be suspended by a court only if serious doubts exist as to their legality; the scope of review may be limited, and tardy objections may be disregarded. Details shall be determined by a law.

(5) Paragraphs (1) to (4) of this Article shall not preclude the conclusion of international agreements of member states of the European Communities with each other or with those third states which, with due regard for the obligations arising from the Convention Relating to the Status of Refugees and the Convention for the Protection of Human Rights and Fundamental Freedoms, whose enforcement must be assured in the contracting states, adopt rules conferring jurisdiction to decide on applications for asylum, including the reciprocal recognition of asylum decisions.

Article 17 [Right of petition]

Every person shall have the right individually or jointly with others to address written requests or complaints to competent authorities and to the legislature.

Article 17a [Restriction of basic rights in specific instances]

(1) Laws regarding military and alternative service may provide that the basic right of members of the Armed Forces and of alternative service freely to express and disseminate their opinions in speech, writing and pictures (first clause of the first sentence of paragraph (1) of Article 5), the basic right of assembly (Article 8) and the right of petition (Article 17), insofar as it permits the submission of requests or complaints jointly with others, be restricted during their period of military or alternative service.

(2) Laws regarding defence, including protection of the civilian population, may provide for restriction of the basic rights of freedom of movement (Article 11) and inviolability of the home (Article 13).

Article 18 [Forfeiture of basic rights]

Whoever abuses the freedom of expression, in particular the freedom of the press (paragraph (1) of Article 5), the freedom of teaching (paragraph (3) of Article 5), the freedom of assembly (Article 8), the freedom of association (Article 9), the privacy of correspondence, posts and telecommunications (Article 10), the rights of property (Article 14) or the right of asylum (Article 16a) in order to combat the free democratic basic order shall forfeit these basic rights. This forfeiture and its extent shall be declared by the Federal Constitutional Court.

Article 19 [Restriction of basic rights – Legal remedies]

(1) Insofar as, under this Basic Law, a basic right may be restricted by or pursuant to a law, such law must apply generally and not merely to a single case. In addition, the law must specify the basic right affected and the Article in which it appears.

(2) In no case may the essence of a basic right be affected.

(3) The basic rights shall also apply to domestic legal persons to the extent that the nature of such rights permits.

(4) Should any person's rights be violated by public authority, he may have recourse to the courts. If no other jurisdiction has been established, recourse shall be to the ordinary courts. The second sentence of paragraph (2) of Article 10 shall not be affected by this paragraph.

II. The Federation and the *Länder*

Article 20 [Constitutional principles – Right of resistance]

(1) The Federal Republic of Germany is a democratic and social federal state.

(2) All state authority is derived from the people. It shall be exercised by the people through elections and other votes and through specific legislative, executive and judicial bodies.

(3) The legislature shall be bound by the constitutional order, the executive and the judiciary by law and justice.

(4) All Germans shall have the right to resist any person seeking to abolish this constitutional order if no other remedy is available.

Article 20a [Protection of the natural foundations of life and animals]

Mindful also of its responsibility towards future generations, the state shall protect the natural foundations of life and animals by legislation and, in accordance with law and justice, by executive and judicial action, all within the framework of the constitutional order.

Article 21 [Political parties]

(1) Political parties shall participate in the formation of the political will of the people. They may be freely established. Their internal organisation must conform to democratic principles. They must publicly account for their assets and for the sources and use of their funds.

(2) Parties that, by reason of their aims or the behaviour of their adherents, seek to undermine or abolish the free democratic basic order or to endanger the existence of the Federal Republic of Germany shall be unconstitutional.

(3) Parties that, by reason of their aims or the behaviour of their adherents, are oriented towards an undermining or abolition of the free democratic basic order or an endangerment of the existence of the Federal Republic of Germany shall be excluded from state financing. If such exclusion is determined, any favourable fiscal treatment of these parties and of payments made to those parties shall cease.

(4) The Federal Constitutional Court shall rule on the question of unconstitutionality within the meaning of paragraph (2) of this Article and on exclusion from state financing within the meaning of paragraph (3).

(5) Details shall be regulated by federal laws.

Article 22 [Federal capital – Federal flag]

(1) Berlin is the capital of the Federal Republic of Germany. The Federation shall be responsible for representing the nation as a whole in the capital. Details shall be regulated by federal law.

(2) The federal flag shall be black, red and gold.

Article 23 [European Union – Protection of basic rights – Principle of subsidiarity]

(1) With a view to establishing a united Europe, the Federal Republic of Germany shall participate in the development of the European Union that is committed to democratic, social and federal principles, to the rule of law and to the principle of subsidiarity and that guarantees a level of protection of basic rights essentially comparable to that afforded by this Basic Law. To this end the Federation may transfer sovereign powers by a law with the consent of the Bundesrat. The establishment of the European Union, as well as changes in its treaty foundations and comparable regulations that amend or supplement this Basic Law or make such amendments or supplements possible, shall be subject to paragraphs (2) and (3) of Article 79.

(1a) The Bundestag and the Bundesrat shall have the right to bring an action before the Court of Justice of the European Union to challenge a legislative act of the European Union for infringing the principle of subsidiarity. The Bundestag is obliged to initiate such an action at the request of one fourth of its Members. By a statute requiring the consent of the Bundesrat, exceptions to the first sentence of paragraph (2) of Article 42 and the first sentence of paragraph (3) of Article 52 may be authorised for the exercise of the rights granted to the Bundestag and the Bundesrat under the contractual foundations of the European Union.

(2) The Bundestag and, through the Bundesrat, the *Länder* shall participate in matters concerning the European Union. The Federal Government shall notify the Bundestag of such matters comprehensively and as early as possible.

(3) Before participating in legislative acts of the European Union, the Federal Government shall provide the Bundestag with an opportunity to state its position. The Federal Government shall take the position of the Bundestag into account during the negotiations. Details shall be regulated by a law.

(4) The Bundesrat shall participate in the decision-making process of the Federation insofar as it would have been competent to do so in a comparable domestic matter or insofar as the subject falls within the domestic competence of the *Länder*.

(5) Insofar as, in an area within the exclusive competence of the Federation, interests of the *Länder* are affected and in other matters, insofar as the Federation has legislative power, the Federal Government shall take the position of the Bundesrat into account. To the extent that the legislative powers of the *Länder*, the structure of *Land* authorities, or *Land* administrative procedures are primarily affected, the position of the Bundesrat shall receive prime consideration in the formation of the political will of the Federation; this process shall be consistent with the responsibility of the Federation for the nation as a whole. In matters that may result in increased expenditures or reduced revenues for the Federation, the consent of the Federal Government shall be required.

(6) When legislative powers exclusive to the *Länder* concerning matters of school education, culture or broadcasting are primarily affected, the exercise of the rights belonging to the Federal Republic of Germany as a member state of the European Union shall be delegated by the Federation to a representative of the *Länder* designated by the Bundesrat. These rights shall be exercised with the participation of, and in coordination with, the Federal Government; their exercise shall be consistent with the responsibility of the Federation for the nation as a whole.

(7) Details regarding paragraphs (4) to (6) of this Article shall be regulated by a law requiring the consent of the Bundesrat.

Article 24 [Transfer of sovereign powers – System of collective security]

(1) The Federation may, by a law, transfer sovereign powers to international organisations.

(1a) Insofar as the *Länder* are competent to exercise state powers and to perform state functions, they may, with the consent of the Federal Government, transfer sovereign powers to transfrontier institutions in neighbouring regions.

(2) With a view to maintaining peace, the Federation may enter into a system of mutual collective security; in doing so it shall consent to such limitations upon its sovereign powers as will bring about and secure a lasting peace in Europe and among the nations of the world.

(3) For the settlement of disputes between states, the Federation shall accede to agreements providing for general, comprehensive and compulsory international arbitration.

Article 25 [Primacy of international law]

The general rules of international law shall be an integral part of federal law. They shall take precedence over the laws and directly create rights and duties for the inhabitants of the federal territory.

Article 26 [Securing international peace]

(1) Acts tending to and undertaken with intent to disturb the peaceful relations between nations, especially to prepare for a war of aggression, shall be unconstitutional. They shall be criminalised.

(2) Weapons designed for warfare may be manufactured, transported or marketed only with the permission of the Federal Government. Details shall be regulated by a federal law.

Article 27 [Merchant fleet]

All German merchant vessels shall constitute a unitary merchant fleet.

Article 28 [*Land* constitutions – Autonomy of municipalities]

(1) The constitutional order in the *Länder* must conform to the principles of a republican, democratic and social state governed by the rule of law within the meaning of this Basic Law. In each *Land*, county and municipality the people shall be represented by a body chosen in general, direct, free, equal and secret elections. In county and municipal elections, persons who possess the citizenship of any member state of the European Community are also eligible to vote and to be elected in accordance with European Community law. In municipalities a local assembly may take the place of an elected body.

(2) Municipalities must be guaranteed the right to regulate all local affairs on their own responsibility within the limits prescribed by the laws. Within the limits of their functions designated by a law, associations of municipalities shall also have the right of self-government in accordance with the laws. The guarantee of self-government shall extend to the bases of financial autonomy; these bases shall include the right of municipalities to a source of tax revenues based upon economic ability and the right to establish the rates at which these sources shall be taxed.

(3) The Federation shall guarantee that the constitutional order of the *Länder* conforms to the basic rights and to the provisions of paragraphs (1) and (2) of this Article.

Article 29 [New delimitation of the federal territory]

(1) The division of the federal territory into *Länder* may be revised to ensure that each *Land* be of a size and capacity to perform its functions effectively. Due regard shall be given in this connection to regional, historical and cultural ties, economic efficiency and the requirements of local and regional planning.

(2) Revisions of the existing division into *Länder* shall be effected by a federal law, which must be confirmed by referendum. The affected *Länder* shall be afforded an opportunity to be heard.

(3) The referendum shall be held in the *Länder* from whose territories or parts of territories a new *Land* or a *Land* with redefined boundaries is to be established (affected *Länder*). The question to be voted on is whether the affected *Länder* are to remain as they are or whether the new *Land* or the *Land* with redefined boundaries should be established. The proposal to establish a new *Land* or a *Land* with redefined boundaries shall take effect if the change is approved by a majority in the future territory of such *Land* and by a majority in the territories or parts of territories of an affected *Land* taken together whose affiliation with a *Land* is to be changed in the same way. The proposal shall not take effect if, within the territory of any of the affected *Länder*, a majority reject the change; however, such rejection shall be of no consequence if in any part of the territory whose affiliation with the affected *Land* is to be changed a two-thirds majority approves the change, unless it is rejected by a two-thirds majority in the territory of the affected *Land* as a whole.

(4) If, in any clearly defined and contiguous residential and economic area located in two or more *Länder* and having at least one million inhabitants, one tenth of those entitled to vote in Bundestag elections petition for the inclusion of that area in a single *Land*, a federal law shall specify within two years whether the change shall be made in accordance with paragraph (2) of this Article or that an advisory referendum shall be held in the affected *Länder*.

(5) The advisory referendum shall establish whether the changes the law proposes meet with the voters' approval. The law may put forward not more than two distinct proposals for consideration by the voters. If a majority approves a proposed change of the existing division into *Länder*, a federal law shall specify within two years whether the change shall be made in accordance with paragraph (2) of this Article. If a proposal is approved in accordance with the third and fourth sentences of paragraph (3) of this Article, a federal law providing for establishment of the proposed *Land* shall be enacted within two years after the advisory ballot, and confirmation by referendum shall no longer be required.

(6) A majority in a referendum or in an advisory referendum shall consist of a majority of the votes cast, provided that it amounts to at least one quarter of those entitled to vote in Bundestag elections. Other details concerning referendums, petitions and advisory referendums shall be regulated by a federal law, which may also provide that the same petition may not be filed more than once within a period of five years.

(7) Other changes concerning the territory of the *Länder* may be effected by agreements between the *Länder* concerned or by a federal law with the consent of the Bundesrat, if the territory that is to be the subject of the change has no more than 50,000 inhabitants. Details shall be regulated by a federal law requiring the consent of the Bundesrat and of a majority of the Members of the Bundestag. The law must provide affected municipalities and counties with an opportunity to be heard.

(8) *Länder* may revise the division of their existing territory or parts of their territory by agreement without regard to the provisions of paragraphs (2) to **(7)** of this Article. Affected municipalities and counties shall be afforded an opportunity to be heard. The agreement shall require confirmation by referendum in each of the *Länder* concerned. If the revision affects only part of a

Land's territory, the referendum may be confined to the areas affected; the second clause of the fifth sentence shall not apply. In a referendum under this paragraph a majority of the votes cast shall be decisive, provided it amounts to at least one quarter of those entitled to vote in Bundestag elections; details shall be regulated by a federal law. The agreement shall require the consent of the Bundestag.

Article 30 [Sovereign powers of the *Länder*]

Except as otherwise provided or permitted by this Basic Law, the exercise of state powers and the discharge of state functions is a matter for the *Länder*.

Article 31 [Supremacy of federal law]

Federal law shall take precedence over *Land* law.

Article 32 [Foreign relations]

(1) Relations with foreign states shall be conducted by the Federation.

(2) Before the conclusion of a treaty affecting the special circumstances of a *Land*, that *Land* shall be consulted in timely fashion.

(3) Insofar as the *Länder* have power to legislate, they may conclude treaties with foreign states with the consent of the Federal Government.

Article 33 [Equal citizenship – Public service]

(1) Every German shall have in every *Land* the same political rights and duties.

(2) Every German shall be equally eligible for any public office according to his aptitude, qualifications and professional achievements.

(3) Neither the enjoyment of civil and political rights nor eligibility for public office nor rights acquired in the public service shall be dependent upon religious affiliation. No one may be disadvantaged by reason of adherence or non-adherence to a particular religious denomination or philosophical creed.

(4) The exercise of sovereign authority on a regular basis shall, as a rule, be entrusted to members of the public service who stand in a relationship of service and loyalty defined by public law.

(5) The law governing the public service shall be regulated and developed with due regard to the traditional principles of the professional civil service.

Article 34 [Liability for violation of official duty]

If any person, in the exercise of a public office entrusted to him, violates his official duty to a third party, liability shall rest principally with the state or public body that employs him. In the event of intentional wrongdoing or gross negligence, the right of recourse against the individual officer shall be preserved. The ordinary courts shall not be closed to claims for compensation or indemnity.

Article 35 [Legal and administrative assistance and assistance during disasters]

(1) All federal and *Land* authorities shall render legal and administrative assistance to one another.

(2) In order to maintain or restore public security or order, a *Land* in particularly serious cases may call upon personnel and facilities of the Federal Border Police to assist its police when without such assistance the police could not fulfil their responsibilities, or could do so only with great difficulty. In order to respond to a grave accident or a natural disaster, a *Land* may call for the assistance of police forces of other *Länder* or of personnel and facilities of other administrative authorities, of the Armed Forces or of the Federal Border Police.

(3) If the natural disaster or accident endangers the territory of more than one *Land*, the Federal Government, insofar as is necessary to combat the danger, may instruct the *Land* governments to place police forces at the disposal of other *Länder* and may deploy units of the Federal Border Police or the Armed

Forces to support the police. Measures taken by the Federal Government pursuant to the first sentence of this paragraph shall be rescinded at any time at the demand of the Bundesrat and in any event as soon as the danger is removed.

Article 36 [Personnel of federal authorities]

(1) Civil servants employed by the highest federal authorities shall be drawn from all *Länder* in appropriate proportion. Persons employed by other federal authorities shall, as a rule, be drawn from the *Land* in which they serve.

(2) Laws regarding military service shall also take into account both the division of the Federation into *Länder* and the regional loyalties of their people.

Article 37 [Federal execution]

(1) If a *Land* fails to comply with its obligations under this Basic Law or other federal laws, the Federal Government, with the consent of the Bundesrat, may take the necessary steps to compel the *Land* to comply with its duties.

(2) For the purpose of implementing such coercive measures, the Federal Government or its representative shall have the right to issue instructions to all *Länder* and their authorities.

III. The Bundestag

Article 38 [Elections]

(1) Members of the German Bundestag shall be elected in general, direct, free, equal and secret elections. They shall be representatives of the whole people, not bound by orders or instructions and responsible only to their conscience.

(2) Any person who has attained the age of eighteen shall be entitled to vote; any person who has attained the age of majority may be elected.

(3) Details shall be regulated by a federal law.

Article 39 [Electoral term – Convening]

(1) Save the following provisions, the Bundestag shall be elected for four years. Its term shall end when a new Bundestag convenes. New elections shall be held no sooner than forty-six months and no later than forty-eight months after the electoral term begins. If the Bundestag is dissolved, new elections shall be held within sixty days.

(2) The Bundestag shall convene no later than the thirtieth day after the elections.

(3) The Bundestag shall determine when its sessions shall be adjourned and resumed. The President of the Bundestag may convene it at an earlier date. He shall be obliged to do so if one third of the Members, the Federal President or the Federal Chancellor so demand.

Article 40 [Presidency – Rules of procedure]

(1) The Bundestag shall elect its President, Vice-Presidents and secretaries. It shall adopt rules of procedure.

(2) The President shall exercise proprietary and police powers in the Bundestag building. No search or seizure may take place on the premises of the Bundestag without his permission.

Article 41 [Scrutiny of elections]

(1) Scrutiny of elections shall be the responsibility of the Bundestag. It shall also decide whether a Member has lost his seat.

(2) Complaints against such decisions of the Bundestag may be lodged with the Federal Constitutional Court.

(3) Details shall be regulated by a federal law.

Article 42 [Public sittings – Majority decisions]

(1) Sittings of the Bundestag shall be public. On the motion of one tenth of its Members, or on the motion of the Federal Government, a decision to exclude the public may be taken by a two-thirds majority. The motion shall be voted upon at a sitting not open to the public.

(2) Decisions of the Bundestag shall require a majority of the votes cast unless this Basic Law otherwise provides. The rules of procedure may permit exceptions with respect to elections to be conducted by the Bundestag.

(3) Truthful reports of public sittings of the Bundestag and of its committees shall not give rise to any liability.

Article 43 [Right to require presence, right of access and right to be heard]

(1) The Bundestag and its committees may require the presence of any member of the Federal Government.

(2) The members of the Bundesrat and of the Federal Government as well as their representatives may attend all sittings of the Bundestag and meetings of its committees. They shall have the right to be heard at any time.

Article 44 [Committees of inquiry]

(1) The Bundestag shall have the right, and on the motion of one quarter of its Members the duty, to establish a committee of inquiry, which shall take the requisite evidence at public hearings. The public may be excluded.

(2) The rules of criminal procedure shall apply, *mutatis mutandis*, to the taking of evidence. The privacy of correspondence, posts and telecommunications shall not be affected.

(3) Courts and administrative authorities shall be required to provide legal and administrative assistance.

(4) The decisions of committees of inquiry shall not be subject to judicial review. The courts shall be free to evaluate and rule upon the facts that were the subject of the investigation.

Article 45 [Committee on the European Union]

The Bundestag shall appoint a Committee on European Union Affairs. It may authorise the committee to exercise the rights of the Bundestag under Article 23 vis-à-vis the Federal Government. It may also empower it to exercise the rights granted to the Bundestag under the contractual foundations of the European Union.

Article 45a [Committees on Foreign Affairs and Defence]

(1) The Bundestag shall appoint a Committee on Foreign Affairs and a Defence Committee.

(2) The Defence Committee shall also have the powers of a committee of inquiry. On the motion of one quarter of its members it shall have the duty to make a specific matter the subject of inquiry.

(3) Paragraph (1) of Article 44 shall not apply to defence matters.

Article 45b [Parliamentary Commissioner for the Armed Forces]

A Parliamentary Commissioner for the Armed Forces shall be appointed to safeguard basic rights and to assist the Bundestag in exercising parliamentary oversight. Details shall be regulated by a federal law.

Article 45c [Petitions Committee]

(1) The Bundestag shall appoint a Petitions Committee to deal with requests and complaints addressed to the Bundestag pursuant to Article 17.

(2) The powers of the Committee to consider complaints shall be regulated by a federal law.

Article 45d Parliamentary Oversight Panel

(1) The Bundestag shall appoint a panel to oversee the intelligence activities of the Federation.

(2) Details shall be regulated by a federal law.

Article 46 [Immunities of Members]

(1) At no time may a Member be subjected to court proceedings or disciplinary action or otherwise called to account outside the Bundestag for a vote cast or a remark made by him in the Bundestag or in any of its committees. This provision shall not apply to defamatory insults.

(2) A Member may not be called to account or arrested for a punishable offence without permission of the Bundestag unless he is apprehended while committing the offence or in the course of the following day.

(3) The permission of the Bundestag shall also be required for any other restriction of a Member's freedom of the person or for the initiation of proceedings against a Member under Article 18.

(4) Any criminal proceedings or any proceedings under Article 18 against a Member and any detention or other restriction of the freedom of his person shall be suspended at the demand of the Bundestag.

Article 47 [Right of refusal to give evidence]

Members may refuse to give evidence concerning persons who have confided information to them in their capacity as Members of the Bundestag or to whom they have confided information in this capacity and to give evidence concerning this information itself. To the extent that this right of refusal to give evidence applies, no seizure of documents shall be permissible.

Article 48 [Candidature – Protection of membership – Remuneration]

(1) Every candidate for election to the Bundestag shall be entitled to the leave necessary for his election campaign.

(2) No one may be prevented from accepting or exercising the office of Member of the Bundestag. No one may be given notice of dismissal or discharged from employment on this ground.

(3) Members shall be entitled to remuneration adequate to ensure their independence. They shall be entitled to the free use of all publicly owned means of transport. Details shall be regulated by a federal law.

Article 49 (repealed)

IV. The Bundesrat

Article 50 [Functions]
The *Länder* shall participate through the Bundesrat in the legislation and administration of the Federation and in matters concerning the European Union.

Article 51 [Composition – Weighted voting]
(1) The Bundesrat shall consist of members of the *Land* governments, which appoint and recall them. Other members of those governments may serve as alternates.

(2) Each *Land* shall have at least three votes; *Länder* with more than two million inhabitants shall have four, *Länder* with more than six million inhabitants five and *Länder* with more than seven million inhabitants six votes.

(3) Each *Land* may appoint as many members as it has votes. The votes of each *Land* may be cast only as a unit and only by Members present or their alternates.

Article 52 [President – Decisions – Rules of procedure]
(1) The Bundesrat shall elect its President for one year.

(2) The President shall convene the Bundesrat. He shall be obliged to do so if the delegates of at least two *Länder* or the Federal Government so demand.

(3) Decisions of the Bundesrat shall require at least a majority of its votes. It shall adopt rules of procedure. Its meetings shall be open to the public. The public may be excluded.

(3a) For matters concerning the European Union the Bundesrat may establish a Chamber for European Affairs, whose decisions shall be considered decisions of the Bundesrat; the number of votes to be uniformly cast by the *Länder* shall be determined by paragraph (2) of Article 51.

(4) Other members or representatives of *Land* governments may serve on committees of the Bundesrat.

Article 53 [Attendance of members of the Federal Government]

The members of the Federal Government shall have the right, and on demand the duty, to participate in meetings of the Bundesrat and of its committees. They shall have the right to be heard at any time. The Bundesrat shall be kept informed by the Federal Government with regard to the conduct of its affairs.

IV.a. The Joint Committee

Article 53a [Composition – Rules of procedure]

(1) The Joint Committee shall consist of Members of the Bundestag and members of the Bundesrat; the Bundestag shall provide two thirds and the Bundesrat one third of the committee members. The Bundestag shall designate Members in proportion to the relative strength of the various parliamentary groups; they may not be members of the Federal Government. Each *Land* shall be represented by a Bundesrat member of its choice; these members shall not be bound by instructions. The establishment of the Joint Committee and its proceedings shall be regulated by rules of procedure to be adopted by the Bundestag and requiring the consent of the Bundesrat.

(2) The Federal Government shall inform the Joint Committee about its plans for a state of defence. The rights of the Bundestag and its committees under paragraph (1) of Article 43 shall not be affected by the provisions of this paragraph.

V. The Federal President

Article 54 [Election – Term of office]

(1) The Federal President shall be elected by the Federal Convention without debate. Any German who is entitled to vote in Bundestag elections and has attained the age of forty may be elected.

(2) The term of office of the Federal President shall be five years. Re-election for a consecutive term shall be permitted only once.

(3) The Federal Convention shall consist of the Members of the Bundestag and an equal number of members elected by the parliamentary assemblies of the *Länder* on the basis of proportional representation.

(4) The Federal Convention shall meet not later than thirty days before the term of office of the Federal President expires or, in the case of premature termination, not later than thirty days after that date. It shall be convened by the President of the Bundestag.

(5) After the expiry of an electoral term, the period specified in the first sentence of paragraph (4) of this Article shall begin when the Bundestag first convenes.

(6) The person receiving the votes of a majority of the members of the Federal Convention shall be elected. If, after two ballots, no candidate has obtained such a majority, the person who receives the largest number of votes on the next ballot shall be elected.

(7) Details shall be regulated by a federal law.

Article 55 [Incompatibilities]

(1) The Federal President may not be a member of the government or of a legislative body of the Federation or of a *Land*.

(2) The Federal President may not hold any other salaried office or engage in any trade or profession or belong to the management or supervisory board of any enterprise conducted for profit.

Article 56 [Oath of office]

On assuming his office, the Federal President shall take the following oath before the assembled Members of the Bundestag and the Bundesrat:

"I swear that I will dedicate my efforts to the well-being of the German people, promote their welfare, protect them from harm, uphold and defend the Basic Law and the laws of the Federation, perform my duties conscientiously and do justice to all. So help me God."

The oath may also be taken without religious affirmation.

Article 57 [Substitution]

If the Federal President is unable to perform his duties, or if his office falls prematurely vacant, the President of the Bundesrat shall exercise his powers.

Article 58 [Countersignature]

Orders and directions of the Federal President shall require for their validity the countersignature of the Federal Chancellor or of the competent Federal Minister. This provision shall not apply to the appointment or dismissal of the Federal Chancellor, the dissolution of the Bundestag under Article 63, or a request made under paragraph (3) of Article 69.

Article 59 [International representation of the Federation]

(1) The Federal President shall represent the Federation in international law. He shall conclude treaties with foreign states on behalf of the Federation. He shall accredit and receive envoys.

(2) Treaties that regulate the political relations of the Federation or relate to subjects of federal legislation shall require the consent or participation, in the form of a federal law, of the bodies responsible in such a case for the enactment of federal law. In the case of executive agreements the provisions concerning the federal administration shall apply, *mutatis mutandis*.

Article 59a (repealed)

Article 60 [Appointment of civil servants – Pardon – Immunity]

(1) The Federal President shall appoint and dismiss federal judges, federal civil servants and commissioned and non-commissioned officers of the Armed Forces, except as may otherwise be provided by a law.

(2) He shall exercise the power to pardon offenders on behalf of the Federation in individual cases.

(3) He may delegate these powers to other authorities.

(4) Paragraphs (2) to (4) of Article 46 shall apply to the Federal President, *mutatis mutandis.*

Article 61 [Impeachment before the Federal Constitutional Court]

(1) The Bundestag or the Bundesrat may impeach the Federal President before the Federal Constitutional Court for wilful violation of this Basic Law or of any other federal law. The motion of impeachment must be supported by at least one quarter of the Members of the Bundestag or one quarter of the votes of the Bundesrat. The decision to impeach shall require a majority of two thirds of the Members of the Bundestag or of two thirds of the votes of the Bundesrat. The case for impeachment shall be presented before the Federal Constitutional Court by a person commissioned by the impeaching body.

(2) If the Federal Constitutional Court finds the Federal President guilty of a wilful violation of this Basic Law or of any other federal law, it may declare that he has forfeited his office. After the Federal President has been impeached, the Court may issue an interim order preventing him from exercising his functions.

VI. The Federal Government

Article 62 [Composition]

The Federal Government shall consist of the Federal Chancellor and the Federal Ministers.

Article 63 [Election of the Federal Chancellor]

(1) The Federal Chancellor shall be elected by the Bundestag without debate on the proposal of the Federal President.

(2) The person who receives the votes of a majority of the Members of the Bundestag shall be elected. The person elected shall be appointed by the Federal President.

(3) If the person proposed by the Federal President is not elected, the Bundestag may elect a Federal Chancellor within fourteen days after the ballot by the votes of more than one half of its Members.

(4) If no Federal Chancellor is elected within this period, a new election shall take place without delay, in which the person who receives the largest number of votes shall be elected. If the person elected receives the votes of a majority of the Members of the Bundestag, the Federal President must appoint him within seven days after the election. If the person elected does not receive such a majority, then within seven days the Federal President shall either appoint him or dissolve the Bundestag.

Article 64 [Appointment and dismissal of Federal Ministers – Oath of office]

(1) Federal Ministers shall be appointed and dismissed by the Federal President upon the proposal of the Federal Chancellor.

(2) On taking office the Federal Chancellor and the Federal Ministers shall take the oath provided for in Article 56 before the Bundestag.

Article 65 [Power to determine policy guidelines – Department and collegiate responsibility]

The Federal Chancellor shall determine and be responsible for the general guidelines of policy. Within these limits each Federal Minister shall conduct the affairs of his department independently and on his own responsibility. The Federal Government shall resolve differences of opinion between Federal Ministers. The Federal Chancellor shall conduct the proceedings of the Federal Government in accordance with rules of procedure adopted by the Government and approved by the Federal President.

Article 65a [Command of the Armed Forces]

(1) Command of the Armed Forces shall be vested in the Federal Minister of Defence.

(2) (repealed)

Article 66 [Incompatibilities]

Neither the Federal Chancellor nor a Federal Minister may hold any other salaried office or engage in any trade or profession or belong to the management or, without the consent of the Bundestag, to the supervisory board of an enterprise conducted for profit.

Article 67 [Vote of no confidence]

(1) The Bundestag may express its lack of confidence in the Federal Chancellor only by electing a successor by the vote of a majority of its Members and requesting the Federal President to dismiss the Federal Chancellor. The Federal President must comply with the request and appoint the person elected.

(2) Forty-eight hours shall elapse between the motion and the election.

Article 68 [Vote of confidence]

(1) If a motion of the Federal Chancellor for a vote of confidence is not supported by the majority of the Members of the Bundestag, the Federal President, upon the proposal of the Federal Chancellor, may dissolve the Bundestag within twenty-one days. The right of dissolution shall lapse as soon as the Bundestag elects another Federal Chancellor by the vote of a majority of its Members.

(2) Forty-eight hours shall elapse between the motion and the vote.

Article 69 [Deputy Federal Chancellor – Term of office]

(1) The Federal Chancellor shall appoint a Federal Minister as his deputy.

(2) The tenure of office of the Federal Chancellor or of a Federal Minister shall end in any event when a new Bundestag convenes; the tenure of office of a Federal Minister shall also end on any other occasion on which the Federal Chancellor ceases to hold office.

(3) At the request of the Federal President the Federal Chancellor, or at the request of the Federal Chancellor or of the Federal President a Federal Minister, shall be obliged to continue to manage the affairs of his office until a successor is appointed.

VII. Federal Legislation and Legislative Procedures

Article 70 [Division of powers between the Federation and the *Länder*]

(1) The *Länder* shall have the right to legislate insofar as this Basic Law does not confer legislative power on the Federation.

(2) The division of authority between the Federation and the *Länder* shall be governed by the provisions of this Basic Law concerning exclusive and concurrent legislative powers.

Article 71 [Exclusive legislative power of the Federation]

On matters within the exclusive legislative power of the Federation, the *Länder* shall have power to legislate only when and to the extent that they are expressly authorised to do so by a federal law.

Article 72 [Concurrent legislative powers]

(1) On matters within the concurrent legislative power, the *Länder* shall have power to legislate so long as and to the extent that the Federation has not exercised its legislative power by enacting a law.

(2) The Federation shall have the right to legislate on matters falling within items 4, 7, 11, 13, 15, 19a, 20, 22, 25 and 26 of paragraph (1) of Article 74, if and to the extent that the establishment of equivalent living conditions throughout the federal territory or the maintenance of legal or economic unity renders federal regulation necessary in the national interest.

(3) If the Federation has made use of its power to legislate, the *Länder* may enact laws at variance with this legislation with respect to:

1. hunting (except for the law on hunting licences);

2. protection of nature and landscape management (except for the general principles governing the protection of nature, the law on protection of plant and animal species or the law on protection of marine life);

3. land distribution;

4. regional planning;

5. management of water resources (except for regulations related to materials or facilities);

6. admission to institutions of higher education and requirements for graduation in such institutions.

Federal laws on these matters shall enter into force no earlier than six months following their promulgation unless otherwise provided with the consent of the Bundesrat. As for the relationship between federal law and law of the *Länder*, the latest law enacted shall take precedence with respect to matters within the scope of the first sentence.

(4) A federal law may provide that federal legislation which is no longer necessary within the meaning of paragraph (2) of this Article may be superseded by *Land* law.

Article 73 [Matters under exclusive legislative power of the Federation]

(1) The Federation shall have exclusive legislative power with respect to:

1. foreign affairs and defence, including protection of the civilian population;

2. citizenship in the Federation;

3. freedom of movement, passports, residency registration and identity cards, immigration, emigration and extradition;

4. currency, money and coinage, weights and measures, and the determination of standards of time;

5. the unity of the customs and trading area, treaties regarding commerce and navigation, the free movement of goods, and the exchange of goods and payments with foreign countries, including customs and border protection;

5a. safeguarding German cultural assets against removal from the country;

6. air transport;

6a. the operation of railways wholly or predominantly owned by the Federation (federal railways), the construction, maintenance and operation of railway lines belonging to federal railways and the levying of charges for the use of these lines;

7. postal and telecommunications services;

8. the legal relations of persons employed by the Federation and by federal corporations under public law;

9. industrial property rights, copyrights and publishing;

9a. protection by the Federal Criminal Police Office against the dangers of international terrorism when a threat transcends the boundary of one *Land*, when responsibility is not clearly assignable to the police authorities of any particular *Land* or when the highest authority of an individual *Land* requests the assumption of federal responsibility;

10. cooperation between the Federation and the *Länder* concerning

(a) criminal police work,

(b) protection of the free democratic basic order, existence and security of the Federation or of a *Land* (protection of the constitution), and

(c) protection against activities within the federal territory which, by the use of force or preparations for the use of force, endanger the external interests of the Federal Republic of Germany, as well as the establishment of a Federal Criminal Police Office and international action to combat crime;

11. statistics for federal purposes;

12. the law on weapons and explosives;

13. benefits for persons disabled by war and for dependents of deceased war victims as well as assistance to former prisoners of war;

14. the production and utilisation of nuclear energy for peaceful purposes, the construction and operation of facilities serving such purposes, protection against hazards arising from the release of nuclear energy or from ionising radiation, and the disposal of radioactive substances.

(2) Laws enacted pursuant to item 9a of paragraph (1) require the consent of the Bundesrat.

Article 74 [Matters under concurrent legislative powers]

(1) Concurrent legislative power shall extend to the following matters:

1. civil law, criminal law, court organisation and procedure (except for the law governing pre-trial detention), the legal profession, notaries and the provision of legal advice;

2. registration of births, deaths and marriages;

3. the law of association;

4. the law relating to residence and establishment of foreign nationals;

4a. (repealed)

5. (repealed)

6. matters concerning refugees and expellees;

7. public welfare (except for the law on social care homes);

8. (repealed)

9. war damage and reparations;

10. war graves and graves of other victims of war or despotism;

11. the law relating to economic matters (mining, industry, energy, crafts, trades, commerce, banking, stock exchanges and private insurance), except for the law on shop closing hours, restaurants, amusement arcades, display of persons, trade fairs, exhibitions and markets;

12. labour law, including the organisation of enterprises, occupational health and safety and employment agencies, as well as social security, including unemployment insurance;

13. the regulation of educational and training grants and the promotion of research;

14. the law regarding expropriation, to the extent relevant to matters enumerated in Articles 73 and 74;

15. the transfer of land, natural resources and means of production to public ownership or other forms of public enterprise;

16. prevention of the abuse of economic power;

17. the promotion of agricultural production and forestry (except for the law on land consolidation), ensuring the adequacy of food supply, the importation and exportation of agricultural and forestry products, deep-sea and coastal fishing and coastal preservation

18. urban real estate transactions, land law (except for laws regarding development fees), and the law on rental subsidies, subsidies for old debts, homebuilding loan premiums, miners' homebuilding and pit villages;

19. measures to combat human and animal diseases which pose a danger to the public or are communicable, admission to the medical profession and to ancillary professions or occupations, as well as the law on pharmacies, medicines, medical products, drugs, narcotics and poisons;

19a. the economic viability of hospitals and the regulation of hospital charges;

20. the law on food products including animals used in their production, the law on alcohol and tobacco, essential commodities and feedstuffs as well as protective measures in connection with the marketing of agricultural and forest seeds and seedlings, the protection of plants against diseases and pests, as well as the protection of animals;

21. maritime and coastal shipping, as well as navigational aids, inland navigation, meteorological services, sea routes and inland waterways used for general traffic;

22. road traffic, motor transport, construction and maintenance of long-distance highways, as well as the collection of tolls for the use of public highways by vehicles and the allocation of the revenue;

23. non-federal railways, except mountain railways;

24. waste disposal, air pollution control, and noise abatement (except for the protection from noise associated with human activity);

25. state liability;

26. medically assisted generation of human life, analysis and modification of genetic information as well as the regulation of organ, tissue and cell transplantation;

27. the statutory rights and duties of civil servants of the *Länder*, the municipalities and other corporations established under public law as well as of the judges in the *Länder*, except for their career regulations, remuneration and pensions;

28. hunting;

29. protection of nature and landscape management;

30. land distribution;

31. regional planning;

32. management of water resources;

33. admission to institutions of higher education and requirements for graduation in such institutions.

(2) Laws enacted pursuant to items 25 and 27 of paragraph (1) shall require the consent of the Bundesrat.

Article 74a (repealed)

Article 75 (repealed)

Article 76 [Bills]

(1) Bills may be introduced in the Bundestag by the Federal Government, by the Bundesrat or from the floor of the Bundestag.

(2) Federal Government bills shall first be submitted to the Bundesrat. The Bundesrat shall be entitled to comment on such bills within six weeks. If for important reasons, especially with respect to the scope of the bill, the Bundesrat demands an extension, the period shall be increased to nine weeks. If in exceptional circumstances the Federal Government, on submitting a bill to the Bundesrat, declares it to be particularly urgent, it may submit the bill to the Bundestag after three weeks or, if the Bundesrat has demanded an extension pursuant to the third sentence of this paragraph, after six weeks, even if it has not yet received the Bundesrat's comments; upon receiving such comments, it shall transmit them to the Bundestag without delay. In the case of bills to amend this Basic Law or to transfer sovereign powers pursuant to Article 23 or 24, the comment period shall be nine weeks; the fourth sentence of this paragraph shall not apply.

(3) Bundesrat bills shall be submitted to the Bundestag by the Federal Government within six weeks. In submitting them the Federal Government shall state its own views. If for important reasons, especially with respect to the scope of the bill, the Federal Government demands an extension, the period shall be increased to nine weeks. If in exceptional circumstances the

Bundesrat declares a bill to be particularly urgent, the period shall be three weeks or, if the Federal Government has demanded an extension pursuant to the third sentence of this paragraph, six weeks. In the case of bills to amend this Basic Law or to transfer sovereign powers pursuant to Article 23 or 24, the comment period shall be nine weeks; the fourth sentence of this paragraph shall not apply. The Bundestag shall consider and vote on bills within a reasonable time.

Article 77 [Legislative procedure – Mediation Committee]

(1) Federal laws shall be adopted by the Bundestag. After their adoption the President of the Bundestag shall forward them to the Bundesrat without delay.

(2) Within three weeks after receiving an adopted bill, the Bundesrat may demand that a committee for joint consideration of bills, composed of Members of the Bundestag and of the Bundesrat, be convened. The composition and proceedings of this committee shall be regulated by rules of procedure adopted by the Bundestag and requiring the consent of the Bundesrat. The members of the Bundesrat on this committee shall not be bound by instructions. When the consent of the Bundesrat is required for a bill to become law, the Bundestag and the Federal Government may likewise demand that such a committee be convened. Should the committee propose any amendment to the adopted bill, the Bundestag shall vote on it a second time.

(2a) Insofar as its consent is required for a bill to become law, the Bundesrat, if no request has been made pursuant to the first sentence of paragraph (2) of this Article or if the mediation proceeding has been completed without a proposal to amend the bill, shall vote on the bill within a reasonable time.

(3) Insofar as its consent is not required for a bill to become law, the Bundesrat, once proceedings under paragraph (2) of this Article are completed, may within two weeks object to a bill adopted by the Bundestag. The time for objection shall begin, in the case described in the last sentence of paragraph (2) of this Article, upon receipt of the bill as re-adopted by the Bundestag, and in all other cases upon receipt of a communication from the chairman of the committee provided for in paragraph (2) of this Article to the effect that the committee's proceedings have been concluded.

(4) If the objection is adopted by the majority of the votes of the Bundesrat, it may be rejected by a decision of the majority of the Members of the Bundestag. If the Bundesrat adopted the objection by a majority of at least two thirds of its votes, its rejection by the Bundestag shall require a two-thirds majority, including at least a majority of the Members of the Bundestag.

Article 78 [Passage of federal laws]

A bill adopted by the Bundestag shall become law if the Bundesrat consents to it or fails to make a demand pursuant to paragraph (2) of Article 77 or fails to enter an objection within the period stipulated in paragraph (3) of Article 77 or withdraws such an objection or if the objection is overridden by the Bundestag.

Article 79 [Amendment of the Basic Law]

(1) This Basic Law may be amended only by a law expressly amending or supplementing its text. In the case of an international treaty regarding a peace settlement, the preparation of a peace settlement or the phasing out of an occupation regime or designed to promote the defence of the Federal Republic, it shall be sufficient, for the purpose of making clear that the provisions of this Basic Law do not preclude the conclusion and entry into force of the treaty, to add language to the Basic Law that merely makes this clarification.

(2) Any such law shall be carried by two thirds of the Members of the Bundestag and two thirds of the votes of the Bundesrat.

(3) Amendments to this Basic Law affecting the division of the Federation into Länder, their participation in principle in the legislative process, or the principles laid down in Articles 1 and 20 shall be inadmissible.

Article 80 [Issuance of statutory instruments]

(1) The Federal Government, a Federal Minister or the *Land* governments may be authorised by a law to issue statutory instruments. The content, purpose and scope of the authority conferred shall be specified in the law. Each statutory instrument shall contain a statement of its legal basis. If the law provides that such authority may be further delegated, such subdelegation shall be effected by statutory instrument.

(2) Unless a federal law otherwise provides, the consent of the Bundesrat shall be required for statutory instruments issued by the Federal Government or a Federal Minister regarding fees or basic principles for the use of postal and telecommunication facilities, basic principles for levying of charges for the use of facilities of federal railways or the construction and operation of railways, as well as for statutory instruments issued pursuant to federal laws that require the consent of the Bundesrat or that are executed by the *Länder* on federal commission or in their own right.

(3) The Bundesrat may submit to the Federal Government drafts of statutory instruments that require its consent.

(4) Insofar as *Land* governments are authorised by or pursuant to federal laws to issue statutory instruments, the *Länder* shall also be entitled to regulate the matter by a law.

Article 80a [State of tension]

(1) If this Basic Law or a federal law regarding defence, including protection of the civilian population, provides that legal provisions may be applied only in accordance with this Article, their application, except when a state of defence has been declared, shall be permissible only after the Bundestag has determined that a state of tension exists or has specifically approved such application. The determination of a state of tension and specific approval in the cases mentioned in the first sentence of paragraph (5) and the second sentence of paragraph (6) of Article 12a shall require a two-thirds majority of the votes cast.

(2) Any measures taken pursuant to legal provisions by virtue of paragraph (1) of this Article shall be rescinded whenever the Bundestag so demands.

(3) Notwithstanding paragraph (1) of this Article, the application of such legal provisions shall also be permissible on the basis of and in accordance with a decision made by an international body within the framework of a treaty of alliance with the approval of the Federal Government. Any measures taken pursuant to this paragraph shall be rescinded whenever the Bundestag, by the vote of a majority of its Members, so demands.

Article 81 [Legislative emergency]

(1) If, in the circumstances described in Article 68, the Bundestag is not dissolved, the Federal President, at the request of the Federal Government and with the consent of the Bundesrat, may declare a state of legislative emergency with respect to a bill, if the Bundestag rejects the bill although the Federal Government has declared it to be urgent. The same shall apply if a bill has been rejected although the Federal Chancellor had combined it with a motion under Article 68.

(2) If, after a state of legislative emergency has been declared, the Bundestag again rejects the bill or adopts it in a version the Federal Government declares unacceptable, the bill shall be deemed to have become law to the extent that it receives the consent of the Bundesrat. The same shall apply if the Bundestag does not pass the bill within four weeks after it is reintroduced.

(3) During the term of office of a Federal Chancellor, any other bill rejected by the Bundestag may become law in accordance with paragraphs (1) and (2) of this Article within a period of six months after the first declaration of a state of legislative emergency. After the expiry of this period, no further declaration of a state of legislative emergency may be made during the term of office of the same Federal Chancellor.

(4) This Basic Law may neither be amended nor abrogated nor suspended in whole or in part by a law enacted pursuant to paragraph (2) of this Article.

Article 82 [Certification – Promulgation – Entry into force]

(1) Laws enacted in accordance with the provisions of this Basic Law shall, after countersignature, be certified by the Federal President and promulgated in the Federal Law Gazette. Statutory instruments shall be certified by the authority that issues them and, unless a law otherwise provides, shall be promulgated in the Federal Law Gazette.

(2) Every law or statutory instrument shall specify the date on which it shall take effect. In the absence of such a provision, it shall take effect on the fourteenth day after the day on which the Federal Law Gazette containing it was published.

VIII. The Execution of Federal Laws and the Federal Administration

Article 83 [Execution by the *Länder*]

The *Länder* shall execute federal laws in their own right insofar as this Basic Law does not otherwise provide or permit.

Article 84 [*Länder* administration – Federal oversight]

(1) Where the *Länder* execute federal laws in their own right, they shall provide for the establishment of the requisite authorities and regulate their administrative procedures. If federal laws provide otherwise, the *Länder* may enact derogating regulations. If a *Land* has enacted a derogating regulation pursuant to the second sentence, subsequent federal statutory provisions regulating the organisation of authorities and their administrative procedure shall not be enacted until at least six months after their promulgation, provided that no other determination has been made with the consent of the Bundesrat. The third sentence of paragraph (2) of Article 72 shall apply, *mutatis*

48

mutandis. In exceptional cases, owing to a special need for uniform federal legislation, the Federation may regulate the administrative procedure with no possibility of separate *Land* legislation. Such laws shall require the consent of the Bundesrat. Federal laws may not entrust municipalities and associations of municipalities with any tasks.

(2) The Federal Government, with the consent of the Bundesrat, may issue general administrative provisions.

(3) The Federal Government shall exercise oversight to ensure that the *Länder* execute federal laws in accordance with the law. For this purpose the Federal Government may send commissioners to the highest *Land* authorities and, with their consent or, where such consent is refused, with the consent of the Bundesrat, also to subordinate authorities.

(4) Should any deficiencies that the Federal Government has identified in the execution of federal laws in the *Länder* not be corrected, the Bundesrat, on application of the Federal Government or of the *Land* concerned, shall decide whether that *Land* has violated the law. The decision of the Bundesrat may be challenged in the Federal Constitutional Court.

(5) With a view to the execution of federal laws, the Federal Government may be authorised by a federal law requiring the consent of the Bundesrat to issue instructions in particular cases. They shall be addressed to the highest *Land* authorities unless the Federal Government considers the matter urgent.

Article 85 [Execution by the *Länder* on federal commission]

(1) Where the *Länder* execute federal laws on federal commission, establishment of the authorities shall remain the concern of the *Länder*, except insofar as federal laws enacted with the consent of the Bundesrat otherwise provide. Federal laws may not entrust municipalities and associations of municipalities with any tasks.

(2) The Federal Government, with the consent of the Bundesrat, may issue general administrative provisions. It may provide for the uniform training of civil servants and other salaried public employees. The heads of intermediate authorities shall be appointed with its approval.

(3) The *Land* authorities shall be subject to instructions from the competent highest federal authorities. Such instructions shall be addressed to the highest *Land* authorities unless the Federal Government considers the matter urgent. Implementation of the instructions shall be ensured by the highest *Land* authorities.

(4) Federal oversight shall extend to the legality and appropriateness of execution. For this purpose the Federal Government may require the submission of reports and documents and send commissioners to all authorities.

Article 86 [Federal administration]

Where the Federation executes laws through its own administrative authorities or through federal corporations or institutions established under public law, the Federal Government shall, insofar as the law in question makes no special stipulation, issue general administrative provisions. The Federal Government shall provide for the establishment of the authorities insofar as the law in question does not otherwise provide.

Article 87 [Matters]

(1) The foreign service, the federal financial administration and, in accordance with the provisions of Article 89, the administration of federal waterways and shipping shall be conducted by federal administrative authorities with their own administrative substructures. A federal law may establish Federal Border Police authorities and central offices for police information and communications, for the criminal police and for the compilation of data for purposes of protection of the constitution and of protection against activities within the federal territory which, through the use of force or acts preparatory to the use of force, endanger the external interests of the Federal Republic of Germany.

(2) Social insurance institutions whose jurisdiction extends beyond the territory of a single *Land* shall be administered as federal corporations under public law. Social insurance institutions whose jurisdiction extends beyond the territory of a single *Land* but not beyond that of three *Länder* shall, notwithstanding the first sentence of this paragraph, be administered as *Land* corporations under public law, if the *Länder* concerned have specified which *Land* shall exercise supervisory authority.

(3) In addition, autonomous federal higher authorities as well as new federal corporations and institutions under public law may be established by a federal law for matters on which the Federation has legislative power. When the Federation is confronted with new responsibilities with respect to matters on which it has legislative power, federal authorities at intermediate and lower levels may be established, with the consent of the Bundesrat and of a majority of the Members of the Bundestag, in cases of urgent need.

Article 87a [Armed Forces]

(1) The Federation shall establish Armed Forces for purposes of defence. Their numerical strength and general organisational structure must be shown in the budget.

(2) Apart from defence, the Armed Forces may be employed only to the extent expressly permitted by this Basic Law.

(3) During a state of defence or a state of tension the Armed Forces shall have the power to protect civilian property and to perform traffic control functions to the extent necessary to accomplish their defence mission. Moreover, during a state of defence or a state of tension, the Armed Forces may also be authorised to support police measures for the protection of civilian property; in this event the Armed Forces shall cooperate with the competent authorities.

(4) In order to avert an imminent danger to the existence or free democratic basic order of the Federation or of a *Land*, the Federal Government, if the conditions referred to in paragraph (2) of Article 91 obtain and forces of the police and the Federal Border Police are insufficient, may employ the Armed Forces to support the police and the Federal Border Police in protecting civilian property and in combating organised armed insurgents. Any such employment of the Armed Forces shall be discontinued if the Bundestag or the Bundesrat so demands.

Article 87b [Federal Defence Administration]

(1) The Federal Defence Administration shall be conducted as a federal administrative authority with its own administrative substructure. It shall have jurisdiction for personnel matters and direct responsibility for satisfaction of the procurement needs of the Armed Forces. Responsibilities connected with pensions for injured persons or with construction work may be assigned to the Federal Defence Administration only by a federal law requiring the consent of the Bundesrat. Such consent shall also be required for any laws to the extent that they empower the Federal Defence Administration to interfere with rights of third parties; this requirement, however, shall not apply in the case of laws regarding personnel matters.

(2) In addition, federal laws concerning defence, including recruitment for military service and protection of the civilian population, may, with the consent of the Bundesrat, provide that they shall be executed, wholly or in part, either by federal administrative authorities with their own administrative substructures or by the *Länder* on federal commission. If such laws are executed by the *Länder* on federal commission, they may, with the consent of the Bundesrat, provide that the powers vested in the Federal Government or in the competent highest federal authorities pursuant to Article 85 be transferred wholly or in part to federal higher authorities; in this event the law may provide that such authorities shall not require the consent of the Bundesrat in issuing general administrative provisions pursuant to the first sentence of paragraph (2) of Article 85.

Article 87c [Production and utilisation of nuclear energy]

Laws enacted under item 14 of paragraph (1) of Article 73 may, with the consent of the Bundesrat, provide that they shall be executed by the *Länder* on federal commission.

Article 87d [Air transport administration]

(1) Air transport administration shall be conducted under federal administration. Air traffic control services may also be provided by foreign air traffic control organisations which are authorised in accordance with European Community law.

(2) By a federal law requiring the consent of the Bundesrat, responsibilities for air transport administration may be delegated to the *Länder* acting on federal commission.

Article 87e [Rail transport administration]

(1) Rail transport with respect to federal railways shall be administered by federal authorities. Responsibilities for rail transport administration may be delegated by a federal law to the *Länder* acting in their own right.

(2) The Federation shall discharge rail transport administration responsibilities assigned to it by a federal law, above and beyond those regarding federal railways.

(3) Federal railways shall be operated as enterprises under private law. They shall remain the property of the Federation to the extent that their activities embrace the construction, maintenance and operation of the lines. The transfer of federal shares in these enterprises under the second sentence of this paragraph shall be effected pursuant to a law; the Federation shall retain a majority of the shares. Details shall be regulated by a federal law.

(4) The Federation shall ensure that, in developing and maintaining the federal railway system as well as in offering services over this system, other than local passenger services, due account is taken of the interests and

especially the transportation needs of the public. Details shall be regulated by a federal law.

(5) Laws enacted pursuant to paragraphs (1) to (4) of this Article shall require the consent of the Bundesrat. The consent of the Bundesrat shall also be required for laws regarding the dissolution, merger or division of federal railway enterprises, the transfer of federal railway lines to third parties or the abandonment of such lines or affecting local passenger services.

Article 87f [Posts and telecommunications]

(1) In accordance with a federal law requiring the consent of the Bundesrat, the Federation shall ensure the availability of adequate and appropriate postal and telecommunications services throughout the federal territory.

(2) Services within the meaning of paragraph (1) of this Article shall be provided as a matter of private enterprise by the firms succeeding to the special trust Deutsche Bundespost and by other private providers. Sovereign functions in the area of posts and telecommunications shall be discharged by federal administrative authorities.

(3) Notwithstanding the second sentence of paragraph (2) of this Article, the Federation, by means of a federal institution under public law, shall discharge particular responsibilities relating to the firms succeeding to the special trust Deutsche Bundespost as prescribed by a federal law.

Article 88 [The Federal Bank – The European Central Bank]

The Federation shall establish a note-issuing and currency bank as the Federal Bank. Within the framework of the European Union, its responsibilities and powers may be transferred to the European Central Bank, which is independent and committed to the overriding goal of assuring price stability.

Article 89 [Federal waterways – Administration of waterways]

(1) The Federation shall be the owner of the former Reich waterways.

(2) The Federation shall administer the federal waterways through its own authorities. It shall exercise those state functions relating to inland shipping which extend beyond the territory of a single *Land*, and those functions relating to maritime shipping, which are conferred on it by a law. Insofar as federal waterways lie within the territory of a single *Land*, the Federation on its application may delegate their administration to that *Land* on federal commission. If a waterway touches the territory of two or more *Länder*, the Federation may commission that *Land* which is designated by the affected *Länder*.

(3) In the administration, development and new construction of waterways, the requirements of *Land* improvement and of water management shall be assured in agreement with the *Länder*.

Article 90 [Federal roads and motorways]

(1) The Federation shall remain the owner of the federal motorways and other federal trunk roads. This ownership shall be inalienable.

(2) The administration of the federal motorways shall be a matter for the federal administrative authorities. The Federation may make use of a company under private law to discharge its responsibilities. This company shall be in the inalienable ownership of the Federation. Third parties shall have no direct or indirect holding in the company and its subsidiaries. Third parties shall have no holdings in the framework of public-private partnerships in road networks comprising the entire federal motorway network or the entire network of other federal trunk roads in a *Land* or significant parts of these networks. Details shall be regulated by a federal law.

(3) The *Länder*, or such self-governing corporate bodies as are competent under *Land* law, shall administer on federal commission the other federal trunk roads.

(4) At the request of a *Land*, the Federation may assume administrative responsibility for the other federal trunk roads insofar as they lie within the territory of that *Land*.

Article 91 [Internal emergency]

(1) In order to avert an imminent danger to the existence or free democratic basic order of the Federation or of a *Land*, a *Land* may call upon police forces of other *Länder*, or upon personnel and facilities of other administrative authorities and of the Federal Border Police.

(2) If the *Land* where such danger is imminent is not itself willing or able to combat the danger, the Federal Government may place the police in that *Land* and the police forces of other *Länder* under its own orders and deploy units of the Federal Border Police. Any such order shall be rescinded once the danger is removed or at any time on the demand of the Bundesrat. If the danger extends beyond the territory of a single *Land*, the Federal Government, insofar as is necessary to combat such danger, may issue instructions to the *Land* governments; the first and second sentences of this paragraph shall not be affected by this provision.

VIII.a. Joint Tasks

Article 91a [Joint tasks – Responsibility for expenditure]

(1) In the following areas the Federation shall participate in the discharge of responsibilities of the *Länder*, provided that such responsibilities are important to society as a whole and that federal participation is necessary for the improvement of living conditions (joint tasks):

1. improvement of regional economic structures;

2. improvement of the agrarian structure and of coastal preservation.

(2) Federal laws enacted with the consent of the Bundesrat shall specify the joint tasks as well as the details of coordination.

(3) In cases to which item 1 of paragraph (1) of this Article applies, the Federation shall finance one half of the expenditure in each *Land*. In cases to which item 2 of paragraph (1) of this Article applies, the Federation shall finance at least one half of the expenditure, and the proportion shall be the same for all

Länder. Details shall be regulated by law. The provision of funds shall be subject to appropriation in the budgets of the Federation and the *Länder.*

Article 91b [Education programmes and promotion of research]

(1) The Federation and the *Länder* may cooperate on the basis of agreements in cases of supraregional importance in the promotion of sciences, research and teaching. Agreements primarily affecting institutions of higher education shall require the consent of all the *Länder.* This provision shall not apply to agreements regarding the construction of research facilities, including large scientific installations.

(2) The Federation and the *Länder* may mutually agree to cooperate for the assessment of the performance of education systems in international comparison and in drafting relevant reports and recommendations.

(3) The apportionment of costs shall be regulated in the pertinent agreement.

Article 91c [Information technology systems]

(1) The Federation and the *Länder* may cooperate in planning, constructing and operating information technology systems needed to discharge their responsibilities.

(2) The Federation and the *Länder* may agree to specify the standards and security requirements necessary for exchanges between their information technology systems. Agreements regarding the bases of cooperation under the first sentence may provide, for individual responsibilities determined by their content and scope, that detailed regulations be enacted with the consent of a qualified majority of the Federation and the *Länder* as laid down in the agreements. They require the consent of the Bundestag and the legislatures of the participating *Länder;* the right to withdraw from these agreements cannot be precluded. The agreements shall also regulate the sharing of costs.

(3) The *Länder* may also agree on the joint operation of information technology systems along with the establishment of installations for that purpose.

(4) To link the information networks of the Federation and the *Länder*, the Federation shall establish a connection network. Details regarding the establishment and the operation of the connection network shall be regulated by a federal law with the consent of the Bundesrat.

(5) Comprehensive access by means of information technology to the administrative services of the Federation and the *Länder* shall be regulated by a federal law with the consent of the Bundesrat.

Article 91d [Comparison of performance]

With a view to ascertaining and improving the performance of their administrations, the Federation and the *Länder* may conduct comparative studies and publish the results thereof.

Article 91e [Cooperation in respect of basic support for persons seeking employment]

(1) In the execution of federal laws in the field of basic support for persons seeking employment, the Federation and the *Länder* or the municipalities and associations of municipalities responsible pursuant to *Land* law shall cooperate as a rule in joint institutions.

(2) The Federation may authorise a limited number of municipalities and associations of municipalities, at their request and with the consent of the highest *Land* authority, to discharge the tasks pursuant to paragraph (1) alone. In this case, the Federation shall bear the necessary expenditures including the administrative expenses for the tasks which are to be discharged by the Federation in the execution of laws pursuant to paragraph (1).

(3) Details shall be regulated by a federal law requiring the consent of the Bundesrat.

IX. The Judiciary

Article 92 [Court organisation]

The judicial power shall be vested in the judges; it shall be exercised by the Federal Constitutional Court, by the federal courts provided for in this Basic Law and by the courts of the *Länder*.

Article 93 [Jurisdiction of the Federal Constitutional Court]

(1) The Federal Constitutional Court shall rule:

1. on the interpretation of this Basic Law in the event of disputes concerning the extent of the rights and duties of a supreme federal body or of other parties vested with rights of their own by this Basic Law or by the rules of procedure of a supreme federal body;

2. in the event of disagreements or doubts concerning the formal or substantive compatibility of federal law or *Land* law with this Basic Law or the compatibility of *Land* law with other federal law on application of the Federal Government, of a *Land* government or of one fourth of the Members of the Bundestag;

2a. in the event of disagreements as to whether a law meets the conditions set out in paragraph (2) of Article 72, on application of the Bundesrat or of the government or legislature of a *Land*;

3. in the event of disagreements concerning the rights and duties of the Federation and the *Länder*, especially in the execution of federal law by the *Länder* and in the exercise of federal oversight;

4. on other disputes involving public law between the Federation and the *Länder*, between different *Länder* or within a *Land*, unless there is recourse to another court;

4a. on constitutional complaints, which may be filed by any person alleging that one of his basic rights or one of his rights under paragraph (4) of Article

20 or under Article 33, 38, 101, 103 or 104 has been infringed by public authority;

4b. on constitutional complaints filed by municipalities or associations of municipalities on the ground that their right to self-government under Article 28 has been infringed by a law; in the case of infringement by a *Land* law, however, only if the law cannot be challenged in the constitutional court of the *Land*;

4c. on constitutional complaints filed by associations concerning their non-recognition as political parties for an election to the Bundestag;

5. in the other instances provided for in this Basic Law.

(2) At the request of the Bundesrat, a *Land* government or the parliamentary assembly of a *Land*, the Federal Constitutional Court shall also rule whether, in cases falling under paragraph (4) of Article 72, the need for a regulation by federal law does not exist any longer or whether, in the cases referred to in item 1 of paragraph (2) of Article 125a, federal law could not be enacted any longer. The Court's determination that the need has ceased to exist or that federal law could no longer be enacted substitutes a federal law according to paragraph (4) of Article 72 or item 2 of paragraph (2) of Article 125a. A request under the first sentence is admissible only if a bill falling under paragraph (4) of Article 72 or the second sentence of paragraph (2) of Article 125a has been rejected by the German Bundestag or if it has not been considered and determined upon within one year or if a similar bill has been rejected by the Bundesrat.

(3) The Federal Constitutional Court shall also rule on such other matters as shall be assigned to it by a federal law.

Article 94 [Composition of the Federal Constitutional Court]

(1) The Federal Constitutional Court shall consist of federal judges and other members. Half the members of the Federal Constitutional Court shall be elected by the Bundestag and half by the Bundesrat. They may not be members of the Bundestag, of the Bundesrat, of the Federal Government or of any of the corresponding bodies of a *Land*.

(2) The organisation and procedure of the Federal Constitutional Court shall be regulated by a federal law, which shall specify in which instances its decisions shall have the force of law. The law may require that all other legal remedies be exhausted before a constitutional complaint may be filed and may provide for a separate proceeding to determine whether the complaint will be accepted for adjudication.

Article 95 [Supreme federal courts]

(1) The Federation shall establish the Federal Court of Justice, the Federal Administrative Court, the Federal Finance Court, the Federal Labour Court and the Federal Social Court as supreme courts of ordinary, administrative, financial, labour and social jurisdiction.

(2) The judges of each of these courts shall be chosen jointly by the competent Federal Minister and a committee for the selection of judges consisting of the competent *Land* ministers and an equal number of members elected by the Bundestag.

(3) A Joint Chamber of the courts specified in paragraph (1) of this Article shall be established to preserve the uniformity of decisions. Details shall be regulated by a federal law.

Article 96 [Other federal courts]

(1) The Federation may establish a federal court for matters concerning industrial property rights.

(2) The Federation may establish federal military criminal courts for the Armed Forces. These courts may exercise criminal jurisdiction only during a state of defence or over members of the Armed Forces serving abroad or on board warships. Details shall be regulated by a federal law. These courts shall be under the aegis of the Federal Minister of Justice. The judges officiating there as their primary occupation shall be persons qualified to hold judicial office.

(3) The supreme court of review from the courts designated in paragraphs (1) and (2) of this Article shall be the Federal Court of Justice.

(4) The Federation may establish federal courts for disciplinary proceedings against, and for proceedings on complaints by, persons in the federal public service.

(5) With the consent of the Bundesrat, a federal law may provide that courts of the *Länder* shall exercise federal jurisdiction over criminal proceedings in the following matters:

1. genocide;

2. crimes against humanity under international criminal law;

3. war crimes;

4. other acts tending to and undertaken with the intent to disturb the peaceful relations between nations (paragraph (1) of Article 26);

5. state security.

Article 97 [Judicial independence]

(1) Judges shall be independent and subject only to the law.

(2) Judges appointed permanently to positions as their primary occupation may be involuntarily dismissed, permanently or temporarily suspended, transferred or retired before the expiry of their term of office only by virtue of judicial decision and only for the reasons and in the manner specified by the laws. The legislature may set age limits for the retirement of judges appointed for life. In the event of changes in the structure of courts or in their districts, judges may be transferred to another court or removed from office, provided they retain their full salary.

Article 98 [Legal status of judges – Impeachment]

(1) The legal status of federal judges shall be regulated by a special federal law.

(2) If a federal judge infringes the principles of this Basic Law or the constitutional order of a *Land* in his official capacity or unofficially, the Federal Constitutional Court, upon application of the Bundestag, may by a two-thirds majority order that the judge be transferred or retired. In the case of an intentional infringement it may order his dismissal.

(3) The legal status of the judges in the *Länder* shall be regulated by special *Land* laws if item 27 of paragraph (1) of Article 74 does not otherwise provide.

(4) The *Länder* may provide that *Land* judges shall be chosen jointly by the *Land* Minister of Justice and a committee for the selection of judges.

(5) The *Länder* may enact provisions regarding *Land* judges that correspond with those of paragraph (2) of this Article. Existing *Land* constitutional law shall not be affected. The decision in cases of judicial impeachment shall rest with the Federal Constitutional Court.

Article 99 [Constitutional disputes within a *Land*]

A *Land* law may assign the adjudication of constitutional disputes within a *Land* to the Federal Constitutional Court and the final decision in matters involving the application of *Land* law to the supreme courts specified in paragraph (1) of Article 95.

Article 100 [Concrete judicial review]

(1) If a court concludes that a law on whose validity its decision depends is unconstitutional, the proceedings shall be stayed, and a decision shall be obtained from the *Land* court with jurisdiction over constitutional disputes where the constitution of a *Land* is held to be violated or from the Federal Constitutional Court where this Basic Law is held to be violated. This provision shall also apply where the Basic Law is held to be violated by *Land* law and where a *Land* law is held to be incompatible with a federal law.

(2) If, in the course of litigation, doubt exists whether a rule of international law is an integral part of federal law and whether it directly creates rights and duties for the individual (Article 25), the court shall obtain a decision from the Federal Constitutional Court.

(3) If the constitutional court of a *Land*, in interpreting this Basic Law, proposes to derogate from a decision of the Federal Constitutional Court or of the constitutional court of another *Land*, it shall obtain a decision from the Federal Constitutional Court.

Article 101 [Ban on extraordinary courts]

(1) Extraordinary courts shall not be allowed. No one may be removed from the jurisdiction of his lawful judge.

(2) Courts for particular fields of law may be established only by a law.

Article 102 [Abolition of capital punishment]

Capital punishment is abolished.

Article 103 [Fair trial]

(1) In the courts every person shall be entitled to a hearing in accordance with law.

(2) An act may be punished only if it was defined by a law as a criminal offence before the act was committed.

(3) No person may be punished for the same act more than once under the general criminal laws.

Article 104 [Deprivation of liberty]

(1) Liberty of the person may be restricted only pursuant to a formal law and only in compliance with the procedures prescribed therein. Persons in custody may not be subjected to mental or physical mistreatment.

(2) Only a judge may rule upon the permissibility or continuation of any deprivation of liberty. If such a deprivation is not based on a judicial order, a judicial decision shall be obtained without delay. The police may hold no one in custody on their own authority beyond the end of the day following that of the arrest. Details shall be regulated by a law.

(3) Any person provisionally detained on suspicion of having committed a criminal offence shall be brought before a judge no later than the day following that of his arrest; the judge shall inform him of the reasons for the arrest, examine him and give him an opportunity to raise objections. The judge shall, without delay, either issue a written arrest warrant setting forth the reasons therefor or order his release.

(4) A relative or a person enjoying the confidence of the person in custody shall be notified without delay of any judicial decision imposing or continuing a deprivation of liberty.

X. Finance

Article 104a [Apportionment of expenditures – Financial system – Liability]

(1) The Federation and the *Länder* shall separately finance the expenditures resulting from the discharge of their respective responsibilities insofar as this Basic Law does not otherwise provide.

(2) Where the *Länder* act on federal commission, the Federation shall finance the resulting expenditures.

(3) Federal laws providing for money grants to be administered by the *Länder* may provide that the Federation shall pay for such grants wholly or in part. If any such law provides that the Federation shall finance one half or more of the expenditure, it shall be executed by the *Länder* on federal commission.

(4) Federal laws that oblige the *Länder* to provide money grants, benefits in kind or comparable services to third parties and which are executed by the *Länder* in their own right or according to the second sentence of paragraph **(3)** on commission of the Federation shall require the consent of the Bundesrat if the expenditure resulting therefrom is to be borne by the *Länder*.

(5) The Federation and the *Länder* shall finance the administrative expenditures incurred by their respective authorities and shall be responsible to one another for ensuring proper administration. Details shall be regulated by a federal law requiring the consent of the Bundesrat.

(6) In accordance with the internal allocation of competencies and responsibilities, the Federation and the *Länder* shall bear the costs entailed by a violation of obligations incumbent on Germany under supranational or international law. In cases of financial corrections by the European Union with effect transcending one specific *Land*, the Federation and the *Länder* shall bear such costs at a ratio of 15 to 85. In such cases, the *Länder* as a whole shall be responsible in solidarity for 35 per cent of the total burden according to a general formula; 50 per cent of the total burden shall be borne by those *Länder* which have caused the encumbrance, adjusted to the size of the amount of the financial means received. Details shall be regulated by a federal law requiring the consent of the Bundesrat.

Article 104b [Financial assistance for investments]

(1) To the extent that this Basic Law confers on it the power to legislate, the Federation may grant the *Länder* financial assistance for particularly important investments by the *Länder* and municipalities (associations of municipalities) which are necessary to:

1. avert a disturbance of the overall economic equilibrium,

2. equalise differing economic capacities within the federal territory, or

3. promote economic growth.

By way of derogation from the first sentence, the Federation may grant financial assistance even outside its field of legislative powers in cases of natural disasters or exceptional emergency situations beyond governmental control and substantially harmful to the state's financial capacity.

(2) Details, especially with respect to the kinds of investments to be promoted, shall be regulated by a federal law requiring the consent of the Bundesrat or by an executive agreement based on the Federal Budget Act. The federal law or executive agreement may contain provisions on the shaping of the respective *Land* programmes for the use of the financial assistance. The criteria for the shaping of the *Land* programmes shall be specified in agreement with the affected *Länder*. To ensure that the funds are used for their intended purpose, the Federal Government may require the submission of reports and documents and conduct surveys of any authorities. The funds from the Federation shall be provided in addition to funds belonging to the *Länder*. The duration of the grants shall be limited, and the grants must be reviewed at regular intervals with respect to the manner in which they are used. The financial assistance must be designed with descending annual contributions.

(3) Upon request, the Bundestag, the Federal Government and the Bundesrat shall be informed about the implementation of such measures and the improvements reached.

Article 104c [Financial assistance for investments in municipal education infrastructure]

The Federation may grant the *Länder* financial assistance for investments of significance to the nation as a whole, and for special limited-term expenditures on the part of the *Länder* and municipalities (associations of municipalities) directly connected with such investments to improve the efficiency of municipal education infrastructure. The first three sentences and the fifth and sixth sentences of paragraph (2), as well as paragraph (3) of Article 104b, shall apply, *mutatis mutandis*. To ensure that the funds are used for their intended purpose, the Federal Government may require the submission of reports and, where circumstances so warrant, documents.

Article 104d [Financial assistance for investments in social housing]

The Federation may grant the *Länder* financial assistance for investments of significance to the nation as a whole on the part of the *Länder* and municipalities (associations of municipalities) in social housing. The first five sentences of paragraph (2), as well as paragraph (3) of Article 104b, shall apply, *mutatis mutandis*.

Article 105 [Distribution of powers regarding tax laws]

(1) The Federation shall have exclusive power to legislate with respect to customs duties and fiscal monopolies.

(2) The Federation shall have concurrent power to legislate with respect to all other taxes the revenue from which accrues to it wholly or in part or as to which the conditions provided for in paragraph (2) of Article 72 apply.

(2a) The *Länder* shall have power to legislate with regard to local taxes on consumption and expenditures so long and insofar as such taxes are not substantially similar to taxes regulated by federal law. They are empowered to determine the rate of the tax on acquisition of real estate.

(3) Federal laws relating to taxes the revenue from which accrues wholly or in part to the *Länder* or to municipalities (associations of municipalities) shall require the consent of the Bundesrat.

Article 106 [Apportionment of tax revenue and yield of fiscal monopolies]

(1) The yield of fiscal monopolies and the revenue from the following taxes shall accrue to the Federation:

1. customs duties;

2. taxes on consumption insofar as they do not accrue to the *Länder* pursuant to paragraph (2), or jointly to the Federation and the *Länder* in accordance with paragraph (3) or to municipalities in accordance with paragraph (6) of this Article;

3. the road freight tax, motor vehicle tax, and other taxes on transactions related to motorised vehicles;

4. the taxes on capital transactions, insurance and bills of exchange;

5. non-recurring levies on property and equalisation of burdens levies;

6. income and corporation surtaxes;

7. levies imposed within the framework of the European Communities.

(2) Revenue from the following taxes shall accrue to the *Länder*:

1. the property tax;

2. the inheritance tax;

3. the motor vehicle tax;

4. such taxes on transactions as do not accrue to the Federation pursuant to paragraph (1) or jointly to the Federation and the *Länder* pursuant to paragraph (3) of this Article;

5. the beer tax;

6. the tax on gambling establishments.

(3) Revenue from income taxes, corporation taxes and turnover taxes shall accrue jointly to the Federation and the *Länder* (joint taxes) to the extent that the revenue from the income tax and the turnover tax is not allocated to municipalities pursuant to paragraphs (5) and (5a) of this Article. The Federation and the *Länder* shall share equally the revenues from income taxes and corporation taxes. The respective shares of the Federation and the *Länder* in the revenue from the turnover tax shall be determined by a federal law requiring the consent of the Bundesrat. Such determination shall be based on the following principles:

1. The Federation and the *Länder* shall have an equal claim against current revenues to cover their necessary expenditures. The extent of such expenditures shall be determined with due regard to multi-year financial planning.

2. The financial requirements of the Federation and of the *Länder* shall be coordinated in such a way as to establish a fair balance, avoid excessive burdens on taxpayers and ensure uniformity of living standards throughout the federal territory.

In determining the respective shares of the Federation and the *Länder* in the revenue from the turnover tax, reductions in revenue incurred by the *Länder* from 1 January 1996 because of the provisions made with respect to children in the income tax law shall also be taken into account. Details shall be regulated by the federal law enacted pursuant to the third sentence of this paragraph.

(4) The respective shares of the Federation and the *Länder* in the revenue from the turnover tax shall be apportioned anew whenever the ratio of revenues to expenditures of the Federation becomes substantially different from that of the *Länder*; reductions in revenue that are taken into account in determining the respective shares of revenue from the turnover tax under the fifth sentence of paragraph (3) of this Article shall not be considered in this regard. If a federal law imposes additional expenditures on or withdraws revenue from the *Länder*, the additional burden may be compensated for by federal grants pursuant to a federal law requiring the consent of the Bundesrat, provided the additional burden is limited to a short period of time. This law shall establish the principles for calculating such grants and distributing them among the *Länder*.

(5) A share of the revenue from the income tax shall accrue to the municipalities, to be passed on by the *Länder* to their municipalities on the basis of the income taxes paid by their inhabitants. Details shall be regulated by a federal law requiring the consent of the Bundesrat. This law may provide that municipalities may establish supplementary or reduced rates with respect to their share of the tax.

(5a) From and after 1 January 1998, a share of the revenue from the turnover tax shall accrue to the municipalities. It shall be passed on by the *Länder* to their municipalities on the basis of a formula reflecting geographical and economic factors. Details shall be regulated by a federal law requiring the consent of the Bundesrat.

(6) Revenue from taxes on real property and trades shall accrue to the municipalities; revenue from local taxes on consumption and expenditures shall accrue to the municipalities or, as may be provided for by *Land* legislation, to associations of municipalities. Municipalities shall be authorised to establish the rates at which taxes on real property and trades are levied, within the framework of the laws. If there are no municipalities in a *Land*, revenue from taxes on real property and trades as well as from local taxes on consumption and expenditures shall accrue to the *Land*. The Federation and the *Länder* may participate, by virtue of an apportionment, in the revenue from the tax on trades. Details regarding such apportionment shall be regulated by a federal law requiring the consent of the Bundesrat. In accordance with *Land* legislation, taxes on real property and trades as well as the municipalities' share of revenue from the income tax and the turnover tax may be taken as a basis for calculating the amount of apportionment.

(7) An overall percentage of the *Land* share of total revenue from joint taxes, to be determined by *Land* legislation, shall accrue to the municipalities or associations of municipalities. In all other respects *Land* legislation shall determine whether and to what extent revenue from *Land* taxes shall accrue to municipalities (associations of municipalities).

(8) If in individual *Länder* or municipalities (associations of municipalities) the Federation requires special facilities to be established that directly result in an increase of expenditure or in reductions in revenue (special burden) to these *Länder* or municipalities (associations of municipalities), the Federation shall grant the necessary compensation if and insofar as the *Länder* or municipalities (associations of municipalities) cannot reasonably be expected to bear the burden. In granting such compensation, due account shall be taken of indemnities paid by third parties and financial benefits accruing to these *Länder* or municipalities (associations of municipalities) as a result of the establishment of such facilities.

(9) For the purpose of this Article, revenues and expenditures of municipalities (associations of municipalities) shall also be deemed to be revenues and expenditures of the *Länder*.

Article 106a [Federal grants for local public transport]

Beginning on 1 January 1996 the *Länder* shall be entitled to an allocation of federal tax revenues for purposes of local public transport. Details shall be regulated by a federal law requiring the consent of the Bundesrat. Allocations made pursuant to the first sentence of this Article shall not be taken into account in determining the financial capacity of a *Land* under paragraph (2) of Article 107.

Article 106b [*Länder* share of motor vehicle tax]

As of 1 July 2009, following the transfer of the motor vehicle tax to the Federation, the *Länder* shall be entitled to a sum from the tax revenue of the Federation. Details shall be regulated by a federal law requiring the consent of the Bundesrat.

Article 107 [Distribution of tax revenue – Financial equalisation among the *Länder* – Supplementary grants]

(1) Revenue from *Land* taxes and the *Land* share of revenue from income and corporation taxes shall accrue to the individual *Länder* to the extent that such taxes are collected by finance authorities within their respective territories (local revenue). Details regarding the delimitation as well as the manner and scope of allotment of local revenue from corporation and wage taxes shall be regulated by a federal law requiring the consent of the Bundesrat. This law may also provide for the delimitation and allotment of local revenue from other taxes. The *Land* share of revenue from the turnover tax shall accrue to the individual *Länder* on a per capita basis, unless otherwise provided in paragraph (2) of this Article.

(2) A federal law requiring the consent of the Bundesrat shall ensure a reasonable equalisation of the disparate financial capacities of the *Länder*, with due regard for the financial capacities and needs of municipalities (associations of municipalities). To this end, additions to and deductions from the financial capacity of the respective *Länder* shall be regulated in the allotment of their shares of revenue from the turnover tax. The conditions for granting additions and imposing reductions as well as the criteria governing the amount of these additions and deductions shall be specified in the law. For the purpose of measuring financial capacity, it shall be permissible to consider only part of the revenue from mining royalties. The law may also provide for grants to be made by the Federation to financially weak *Länder* from its own funds to assist them in meeting their general financial needs (supplementary grants). Irrespective of the criteria specified in the first to the third sentence of this paragraph, grants may also be made to such financially weak *Länder* whose municipalities (associations of municipalities) have a particularly low capacity to generate tax revenue (municipal tax-base grants) and, in addition, to such financially weak *Länder* whose shares of the support funds under Article 91b are lower than their per capita shares.

Article 108 [Financial administration of the Federation and the *Länder* – Financial courts]

(1) Customs duties, fiscal monopolies, taxes on consumption regulated by a federal law, including the turnover tax on imports, the motor vehicle tax and other transaction taxes related to motorised vehicles as from 1 July 2009 and charges imposed within the framework of the European Communities shall be administered by federal finance authorities. The organisation of these authorities shall be regulated by a federal law. Inasmuch as intermediate authorities have been established, their heads shall be appointed in consultation with the *Land* governments.

(2) All other taxes shall be administered by the financial authorities of the *Länder*. The organisation of these authorities and the uniform training of their civil servants may be regulated by a federal law requiring the consent of the Bundesrat. Inasmuch as intermediate authorities have been established, their heads shall be appointed in agreement with the Federal Government.

(3) Where taxes accruing wholly or in part to the Federation are administered by revenue authorities of the *Länder*, those authorities shall act on federal commission. Paragraphs (3) and (4) of Article 85 shall apply, the Federal Minister of Finance acting in place of the Federal Government.

(4) Where and to the extent that execution of the tax laws will be substantially facilitated or improved thereby, a federal law requiring the consent of the Bundesrat may provide for collaboration between federal and *Land* revenue authorities in matters of tax administration, for the administration of taxes enumerated in paragraph (1) of this Article by revenue authorities of the *Länder* or for the administration of other taxes by federal revenue authorities. The functions of *Land* revenue authorities in the administration of taxes whose revenue accrues exclusively to municipalities (associations of municipalities) may be delegated by the *Länder* to municipalities (associations of municipalities) wholly or in part. The federal law referred to in the first sentence of this paragraph may, with regard to collaboration between the Federation and *Länder*, provide that, with the consent of a majority specified in the law, rules for the execution of tax laws will become binding for all *Länder*.

(4a) A federal law requiring the consent of the Bundesrat may provide, in the case of the administration of taxes enumerated in paragraph (2), for collaboration between *Land* revenue authorities and for an inter-*Land* transfer of

74

competence to *Land* revenue authorities of one or more *Länder* by agreement with the *Länder* concerned where and to the extent that execution of the tax laws will be substantially facilitated or improved thereby. The apportionment of costs may be regulated by a federal law.

(5) The procedures to be followed by federal revenue authorities shall be prescribed by a federal law. The procedures to be followed by *Land* revenue authorities or, as provided by the second sentence of paragraph (4) of this Article, by municipalities (associations of municipalities) may be prescribed by a federal law requiring the consent of the Bundesrat.

(6) Financial jurisdiction shall be uniformly regulated by a federal law.

(7) The Federal Government may issue general administrative rules which, to the extent that administration is entrusted to *Land* revenue authorities or to municipalities (associations of municipalities), shall require the consent of the Bundesrat.

Article 109 [Budget management in the Federation and the *Länder*]

(1) The Federation and the *Länder* shall be autonomous and independent of **one another in the management of their respective budgets.**

(2) The Federation and the *Länder* shall jointly discharge the obligations of the Federal Republic of Germany resulting from legal acts of the European Community for the maintenance of budgetary discipline pursuant to Article 104 of the Treaty Establishing the European Community and shall, within this framework, give due regard to the requirements of overall economic equilibrium.

(3) The budgets of the Federation and the *Länder* shall, in principle, be balanced without revenue from credits. The Federation and *Länder* may introduce rules intended to take into account, symmetrically in times of upswing and downswing, the effects of market developments that deviate from normal conditions, as well as exceptions for natural disasters or unusual emergency situations beyond governmental control and substantially harmful to the

state's financial capacity. For such exceptional regimes, a corresponding amortisation plan must be adopted. Details for the budget of the Federation shall be governed by Article 115 with the proviso that the first sentence shall be deemed to be satisfied if revenue from credits does not exceed 0.35 per cent in relation to the nominal gross domestic product. The *Länder* themselves shall regulate details for the budgets within the framework
of their constitutional powers, the proviso being that the first sentence shall only be deemed to be satisfied if no revenue from credits is admitted.

(4) A federal law requiring the consent of the Bundesrat may establish principles applicable to both the Federation and the *Länder* governing budgetary law, cyclically appropriate budgetary management and long-term financial planning.

(5) Sanctions imposed by the European Community on the basis of the provisions of Article 104 of the Treaty Establishing the European Community in the interest of maintaining budgetary discipline shall be borne by the Federation and the *Länder* at a ratio of 65 to 35 per cent. In solidarity, the *Länder* as a whole shall bear 35 per cent of the charges incumbent on the *Länder* according to the number of their inhabitants; 65 per cent of the charges incumbent on the *Länder* shall be borne by the *Länder* according to their degree of causation. Details shall be regulated by a federal law which shall require the consent of the Bundesrat.

Article 109a [Budgetary emergencies]

(1) To avoid a budgetary emergency, a federal law requiring the consent of the Bundesrat shall provide for:

1. the continuing supervision of budgetary management of the Federation and the *Länder* by a joint body (Stability Council),

2. the conditions and procedures for ascertaining the threat of a budgetary emergency,

3. the principles for the establishment and administration of programs for taking care of budgetary emergencies.

(2) From the year 2020, oversight of compliance with the provisions of paragraph (3) of Article 109 by the Federation and the *Länder* shall be entrusted to the Stability Council. This oversight shall be focused on the provisions and procedures regarding adherence to budgetary discipline from legal acts based on the Treaty on the Functioning of the European Union.

(3) The decisions of the Stability Council and the accompanying documents shall be published.

Article 110 [Federal budget]

(1) All revenues and expenditures of the Federation shall be included in the budget; in the case of federal enterprises and special trusts, only payments to or remittances from them need be included. The budget shall be balanced with respect to revenues and expenditures.

(2) The budget for one or more fiscal years shall be set forth in a law enacted before the beginning of the first year and making separate provision for each year. The law may provide that various parts of the budget apply to different periods of time, divided by fiscal years.

(3) Bills to comply with the first sentence of paragraph (2) of this Article as well as bills to amend the Budget Act or the budget itself shall be submitted simultaneously to the Bundesrat and to the Bundestag; the Bundesrat shall be entitled to comment on such bills within six weeks or, in the case of amending bills, within three weeks.

(4) The Budget Act may contain only such provisions as relate to federal revenues and expenditures and to the period for which it is enacted. The Budget Act may specify that its provisions shall expire only upon promulgation of the next Budget Act or, in the event of an authorisation pursuant to Article 115, at a later date.

Article 111 [Interim budget management]

(1) If, by the end of a fiscal year, the budget for the following year has not been adopted by a law, the Federal Government, until such law comes into force, may make all expenditures that are necessary:

(a) to maintain institutions established by a law and to carry out measures authorised by a law;

(b) to meet the legal obligations of the Federation;

(c) to continue construction projects, procurements and the provision of other benefits or services or to continue to make grants for these purposes, to the extent that amounts have already been appropriated in the budget of a previous year.

(2) To the extent that revenues based upon specific laws and derived from taxes or duties or other sources or the working capital reserves do not cover the expenditures referred to in paragraph (1) of this Article, the Federal Government may borrow the funds necessary to sustain current operations up to a maximum of one quarter of the total amount of the previous budget.

Article 112 [Extrabudgetary expenditures]

Expenditures in excess of budgetary appropriations or for purposes not contemplated by the budget shall require the consent of the Federal Minister of Finance. Such consent may be given only in the event of an unforeseen and unavoidable necessity. Details may be regulated by a federal law.

Article 113 [Increase of expenditures]

(1) Laws that increase the budget expenditures proposed by the Federal Government or entail or will bring about new expenditures shall require the consent of the Federal Government. This requirement shall also apply to laws that entail or will bring about decreases in revenue. The Federal Government may demand that the Bundestag postpone its vote on bills to this effect. In this event the Federal Government shall submit its comments to the Bundestag within six weeks.

(2) Within four weeks after the Bundestag has adopted such a law, the Federal Government may demand that it vote on the law a second time.

(3) If the bill has become law pursuant to Article 78, the Federal Government may withhold its consent only within six weeks and only after having initiated the procedure provided for in the third and fourth sentences of paragraph (1) or in paragraph (2) of this Article. Upon the expiry of this period such consent shall be deemed to have been given.

Article 114 [Submission and auditing of accounts]

(1) For the purpose of discharging the Federal Government, the Federal Minister of Finance shall submit annually to the Bundestag and to the Bundesrat an account for the preceding fiscal year of all revenues and expenditures as well as of assets and debts.

(2) The Federal Court of Audit, whose members shall enjoy judicial independence, shall audit the account and determine whether public finances have been properly and efficiently administered by the Federation. For the purpose of the audit pursuant to the first sentence of this paragraph, the Federal Court of Audit may also conduct surveys of authorities outside the federal administration; this shall also apply in cases in which the Federation allocates to the *Länder* ring-fenced financing for the performance of tasks incumbent on the *Länder*. It shall submit an annual report directly to the Bundestag and the Bundesrat as well as to the Federal Government. In other respects the powers of the Federal Court of Audit shall be regulated by a federal law.

Article 115 [Limits of borrowing]

(1) The borrowing of funds and the assumption of surety obligations, guarantees or other commitments that may lead to expenditures in future fiscal years shall require authorisation by a federal law specifying or permitting computation of the amounts involved.

(2) Revenues and expenditures shall in principle be balanced without revenue from credits. This principle shall be satisfied when revenue obtained by the borrowing of funds does not exceed 0.35 per cent in relation to the nominal gross domestic product. In addition, when economic developments deviate from normal conditions, effects on the budget in periods of upswing and downswing must be taken into account symmetrically. Deviations of actual borrowing from the credit limits specified under the first to third sentences are to be recorded on a control account; debits exceeding the threshold of 1.5 per cent in relation to the nominal gross domestic product are to be reduced in accordance with the economic cycle. The regulation of details, especially the adjustment of revenue and expenditures with regard to financial transactions and the procedure for the calculation of the yearly limit on net borrowing, taking into account the economic cycle on the basis of a procedure for adjusting the cycle together with the control and balancing of deviations of actual borrowing from the credit limit, requires a federal law. In cases of natural catastrophes or unusual emergency situations beyond governmental control and substantially harmful to the state's financial capacity, these credit limits may be exceeded on the basis of a decision taken by a majority of the Members of the Bundestag. The decision must be combined with an amortisation plan. Repayment of the credits borrowed under the sixth sentence must be accomplished within an appropriate period of time.

X.a. State of Defence

Article 115a [Declaration of a state of defence]
(1) Any determination that the federal territory is under attack by armed force or imminently threatened with such an attack (state of defence) shall be made by the Bundestag with the consent of the Bundesrat. Such determination shall

be made on application of the Federal Government and shall require a two-thirds majority of the votes cast, which shall include at least a majority of the Members of the Bundestag.

(2) If the situation imperatively calls for immediate action and if insurmountable obstacles prevent the timely convening of the Bundestag or the Bundestag cannot muster a quorum, the Joint Committee shall make this determination by a two-thirds majority of the votes cast, which shall include at least a majority of its members.

(3) The determination shall be promulgated by the Federal President in the Federal Law Gazette pursuant to Article 82. If this cannot be done in time, promulgation shall be effected in another manner; the determination shall be printed in the Federal Law Gazette as soon as circumstances permit.

(4) If the federal territory is under attack by armed force, and if the competent federal authorities are not in a position at once to make the determination provided for in the first sentence of paragraph (1) of this Article, the determination shall be deemed to have been made and promulgated at the time the attack began. The Federal President shall announce that time as soon as circumstances permit.

(5) If the determination of a state of defence has been promulgated, and if the federal territory is under attack by armed force, the Federal President, with the consent of the Bundestag, may issue declarations under international law regarding the existence of the state of defence. Under the conditions specified in paragraph (2) of this Article, the Joint Committee shall act in place of the Bundestag.

Article 115b [Power of command of the Federal Chancellor]
Upon the promulgation of a state of defence the power of command over the Armed Forces shall pass to the Federal Chancellor.

Article 115c [Extension of the legislative powers of the Federation]

(1) The Federation shall have the right to legislate concurrently for a state of defence even with respect to matters within the legislative powers of the *Länder*. Such laws shall require the consent of the Bundesrat.

(2) To the extent required by circumstances during a state of defence, a federal law for a state of defence may:

1. make temporary provisions concerning compensation in the event of expropriation that deviate from the requirements of the second sentence of paragraph (3) of Article 14;

2. establish a time limit for deprivations of freedom different from that specified in the third sentence of paragraph (2) and the first sentence of paragraph (3) of Article 104, but not exceeding four days, for cases in which no judge has been able to act within the time limit that normally applies.

(3) To the extent necessary to repel an existing or imminently threatened attack, a federal law for a state of defence may, with the consent of the Bundesrat, regulate the administration and finances of the Federation and the *Länder* without regard to Titles VIII, VIIIa and X of this Basic Law, provided that the viability of the *Länder*, municipalities, and associations of municipalities, especially with respect to financial matters, is assured.

(4) Federal laws enacted pursuant to paragraph (1) or item 1 of paragraph (2) of this Article may, for the purpose of preparing for their enforcement, be applied even before a state of defence arises.

Article 115d [Urgent bills]

(1) During a state of defence the federal legislative process shall be governed by the provisions of paragraphs (2) and (3) of this Article without regard to the provisions of paragraph (2) of Article 76, the second sentence of paragraph (1) and paragraphs (2) to (4) of Article 77, Article 78 and paragraph (1) of Article 82.

(2) Federal Government bills that the Government designates as urgent shall be forwarded to the Bundesrat at the same time as they are submitted to the Bundestag. The Bundestag and the Bundesrat shall debate such bills in joint session without delay. Insofar as the consent of the Bundesrat is necessary for any such bill to become law, a majority of its votes shall be required. Details shall be regulated by rules of procedure adopted by the Bundestag and requiring the consent of the Bundesrat.

(3) The second sentence of paragraph (3) of Article 115a shall apply to the promulgation of such laws, *mutatis mutandis.*

Article 115e [Joint Committee]

(1) If, during a state of defence, the Joint Committee by a two-thirds majority of the votes cast, which shall include at least a majority of its members, determines that insurmountable obstacles prevent the timely convening of the Bundestag or that the Bundestag cannot muster a quorum, the Joint Committee shall occupy the position of both the Bundestag and the Bundesrat and shall exercise their powers as a single body.

(2) This Basic Law may neither be amended nor abrogated nor suspended in whole or in part by a law enacted by the Joint Committee. The Joint Committee shall have no power to enact laws pursuant to the second sentence of paragraph (1) of Article 23, paragraph (1) of Article 24 or Article 29.

Article 115f [Use of Federal Border Police – Extended powers of instruction]

(1) During a state of defence the Federal Government, to the extent that circumstances require, may:

1. employ the Federal Border Police throughout the federal territory;

2. issue instructions not only to federal administrative authorities but also to *Land* governments and, if it deems the matter urgent, to *Land* authorities and may delegate this power to members of *Land* governments designated by it.

(2) The Bundestag, the Bundesrat and the Joint Committee shall be informed without delay of the measures taken in accordance with paragraph (1) of this Article.

Article 115g [Federal Constitutional Court]

Neither the constitutional status nor the performance of the constitutional functions of the Federal Constitutional Court or its judges may be impaired. The law governing the Federal Constitutional Court may be amended by a law enacted by the Joint Committee only insofar as the Federal Constitutional Court agrees is necessary to ensure that it can continue to perform its functions. Pending the enactment of such a law, the Federal Constitutional Court may take such measures as are necessary to this end. Determinations by the Federal Constitutional Court pursuant to the second and third sentences of this Article shall be made by a majority of the judges present.

Article 115h [Expiry of electoral terms and terms of office]

(1) Any electoral terms of the Bundestag or of parliamentary assemblies of the *Länder* that are due to expire during a state of defence shall end six months after the termination of the state of defence. A term of office of the Federal President that is due to expire during a state of defence and the exercise of his functions by the President of the Bundesrat in case of the premature vacancy of his office shall end nine months after the termination of the state of defence. The term of office of a member of the Federal Constitutional Court that is due to expire during a state of defence shall end six months after the termination of the state of defence.

(2) Should it be necessary for the Joint Committee to elect a new Federal Chancellor, it shall do so by the votes of a majority of its members; the Federal President shall propose a candidate to the Joint Committee. The Joint Committee may express its lack of confidence in the Federal Chancellor only by electing a successor by a two-thirds majority of its members.

(3) The Bundestag shall not be dissolved while a state of defence exists.

Article 115i [Powers of the *Land* governments]

(1) If the competent federal bodies are not in a position to take the measures necessary to avert the danger, and if the situation imperatively calls for immediate independent action in particular areas of the federal territory, the *Land* governments or the authorities or representatives they designate shall be authorised, within their respective spheres of competence, to take the measures provided for in paragraph (1) of Article 115f.

(2) Any measures taken in accordance with paragraph (1) of this Article may be rescinded at any time by the Federal Government, or, with respect to *Land* authorities and subordinate federal authorities, by Minister-Presidents of the *Länder*.

Article 115k [Rank and duration of emergency provisions]

(1) Laws enacted in accordance with Articles 115c, 115e and 115g, as well as statutory instruments issued on the basis of such laws, shall suspend the operation of incompatible law so long as they are in effect. This provision shall not apply to earlier law enacted pursuant to Articles 115c, 115e or 115g.

(2) Laws adopted by the Joint Committee, as well as statutory instruments issued on the basis of such laws, shall cease to have effect no later than six months after the termination of a state of defence.

(3) Laws containing provisions that diverge from Articles 91a, 91b, 104a, 106 and 107 shall apply no longer than the end of the second fiscal year following the termination of a state of defence. After such termination they may, with the consent of the Bundesrat, be amended by a federal law so as to revert to the provisions of Titles VIIIa and X.

Article 115l [Repeal of emergency measures – Conclusion of peace]

(1) The Bundestag, with the consent of the Bundesrat, may at any time repeal laws enacted by the Joint Committee. The Bundesrat may demand that the Bundestag reach a decision on this question. Any measures taken by the Joint Committee or by the Federal Government to avert a danger shall be rescinded if the Bundestag and the Bundesrat so decide.

(2) The Bundestag, with the consent of the Bundesrat, may at any time, by a decision to be promulgated by the Federal President, declare a state of defence terminated. The Bundesrat may demand that the Bundestag reach a decision on this question. A state of defence shall be declared terminated without delay if the conditions for determining it no longer exist.

(3) The conclusion of peace shall be determined by a federal law.

XI. Transitional and Concluding Provisions

Article 116 [Definition of "German" – Restoration of citizenship]

(1) Unless otherwise provided by a law, a German within the meaning of this Basic Law is a person who possesses German citizenship or who has been admitted to the territory of the German Reich within the boundaries of 31 December 1937 as a refugee or expellee of German ethnic origin or as the spouse or descendant of such person.

(2) Former German citizens who, between 30 January 1933 and 8 May 1945, were deprived of their citizenship on political, racial or religious grounds and their descendants shall, on application, have their citizenship restored. They shall be deemed never to have been deprived of their citizenship if they have established their domicile in Germany after 8 May 1945 and have not expressed a contrary intention.

Article 117 [Suspended entry into force of two basic rights]

(1) Law which is inconsistent with paragraph (2) of Article 3 of this Basic Law shall remain in force until adapted to that provision, but not beyond 31 March 1953.

(2) Laws that restrict freedom of movement in view of the present accommodation shortage shall remain in force until repealed by a federal law.

Article 118 [New delimitation of Baden and Württemberg]

The division of the territory comprising Baden, Württemberg-Baden and Württemberg-Hohenzollern into *Länder* may be revised, without regard to the provisions of Article 29, by agreement between the *Länder* concerned. If no agreement is reached, the revision shall be effected by a federal law, which shall provide for an advisory referendum.

Article 118a [New delimitation of Berlin and Brandenburg]

The division of the territory comprising Berlin and Brandenburg into *Länder* may be revised, without regard to the provisions of Article 29, by agreement between the two *Länder* with the participation of their inhabitants who are entitled to vote.

Article 119 [Refugees and expellees]

In matters relating to refugees and expellees, especially as regards their distribution among the *Länder*, the Federal Government, with the consent of the Bundesrat, may issue statutory instruments having the force of law, pending settlement of the matter by a federal law. In this connection the Federal Government may be authorised to issue individual instructions in particular cases. Unless time is of the essence, such instructions shall be addressed to the highest *Land* authorities.

Article 120 [Occupation costs – Burdens resulting from the war]

(1) The Federation shall finance the expenditures for occupation costs and other internal and external burdens resulting from the war, as regulated in detail by federal laws. To the extent that these war burdens were regulated by federal laws on or before 1 October 1969, the Federation and the *Länder* shall finance such expenditures in the proportion established by such federal laws. Insofar as expenditures for such of these war burdens as neither have been nor will be regulated by federal laws were met on or before 1 October 1965 by *Länder*, municipalities (associations of municipalities) or other entities performing functions of the *Länder* or municipalities, the Federation shall not be obliged to finance them even after that date. The Federation shall be responsible for subsidies towards meeting the costs of social security, including unemployment insurance and public assistance to the unemployed. The distribution of war burdens between the Federation and the *Länder* prescribed by this paragraph shall not be construed to affect any law regarding claims for compensation for consequences of the war.

(2) Revenue shall pass to the Federation at the time it assumes responsibility for the expenditures referred to in this Article.

Article 120a [Equalisation of burdens]

(1) Laws implementing the equalisation of burdens may, with the consent of the Bundesrat, provide that, with respect to equalisation payments, they shall be executed partly by the Federation and partly by the *Länder* acting on federal commission and that the relevant powers vested in the Federal Government and the competent highest federal authorities by virtue of Article 85 shall be wholly or partly delegated to the Federal Equalisation of Burdens Office. In exercising these powers, the Federal Equalisation of Burdens Office shall not require the consent of the Bundesrat; except in urgent cases, its instructions shall be given to the highest *Land* authorities (*Land* Equalisation of Burdens Offices).

(2) The second sentence of paragraph (3) of Article 87 shall not be affected by this provision.

Article 121 [Definition of "majority of the members"]
Within the meaning of this Basic Law, a majority of the Members of the Bundestag and a majority of the members of the Federal Convention shall be a majority of the number of their members specified by a law.

Article 122 [Date of transmission of legislative powers]
(1) From the date on which the Bundestag first convenes, laws shall be enacted only by the legislative bodies recognised by this Basic Law.

(2) Legislative bodies and institutions participating in the legislative process in an advisory capacity whose competence expires by virtue of paragraph (1) of this Article shall be dissolved as of that date.

Article 123 [Continued applicability of pre-existing law]
(1) Law in force before the Bundestag first convenes shall remain in force insofar as it does not conflict with this Basic Law.

(2) Subject to all rights and objections of interested parties, treaties concluded by the German Reich concerning matters within the legislative competence of the *Länder* under this Basic Law shall remain in force, provided they are and continue to be valid under general principles of law, until new treaties are concluded by the authorities competent under this Basic Law or until they are in some other way terminated pursuant to their provisions.

Article 124 [Continued applicability of law within the scope of exclusive legislative power]
Law regarding matters subject to the exclusive legislative power of the Federation shall become federal law in the area in which it applies.

Article 125 [Continued applicability of law within the scope of concurrent legislative power]

Law regarding matters subject to the concurrent legislative power of the Federation shall become federal law in the area in which it applies:

1. insofar as it applies uniformly within one or more occupation zones;

2. insofar as it is law by which former Reich law has been amended since 8 May 1945.

Article 125a [Continued applicability of federal law – Replacement by *Land* law]

(1) Law that was enacted as federal law but that, by virtue of the amendment of paragraph (1) of Article 74, the insertion of the seventh sentence of paragraph (1) of Article 84, of the second sentence of paragraph (1) of Article 85 or of the second sentence of paragraph (2a) of Article 105 or because of the repeal of Articles 74a, 75 or the second sentence of paragraph (3) of Article 98, could no longer be enacted as federal law shall remain in force as federal law. It may be superseded by *Land* law.

(2) Law that was enacted pursuant to paragraph (2) of Article 72 as it stood up to 15 November 1994 but which, because of the amendment of paragraph (2) of Article 72, could no longer be enacted as federal law shall remain in force as federal law. A federal law may provide that it may be superseded by *Land* law.

(3) Law that has been enacted as *Land* law but which, because of the amendment of Article 73, could not be enacted any longer as *Land* law shall continue in force as *Land* law. It may be superseded by federal law.

Article 125b [Continued applicability of framework laws – Deviation power of the *Länder*]

(1) Law that was enacted pursuant to Article 75 as it stood up to 1 September 2006 and which could be enacted as federal law even after this date shall remain in force as federal law. The powers and duties of the *Länder* to legis-late shall, in this regard, remain unaffected. In the areas referred to in the first sentence of paragraph (3) of Article 72 the *Länder* may enact regulations that deviate from this law; however, in those areas covered by items 2, 5 and 6 of the first sentence of Article 72 the *Länder* may do so only if and insofar as the Federation has made use of its power to legislate after 1 September 2006, in those areas covered by items 2 and 5 beginning at the latest on 1 January 2010, in cases under item 6 beginning at the latest on 1 August 2008.

(2) The *Länder* may enact regulations derogating from federal regulations enacted pursuant to paragraph (1) of Article 84 as it stood up to 1 September 2006; up to 31 December 2008, however, they may derogate from regulations on administrative procedure only if, after 1 September 2006, regulations on administrative procedure in the relevant federal law have been amended.

Article 125c [Continued applicability of law within the scope of joint tasks]

(1) Law that was enacted by virtue of paragraph (2) of Article 91a in conjunc-tion with item 1 of paragraph (1) as it stood up to 1 September 2006 shall continue in force until 31 December 2006.

(2) The rules enacted in the areas of municipal transport financing and pro-motion of social housing by virtue of paragraph (4) of Article 104a as it stood up to 1 September 2006 shall remain in force until 31 December 2006. The rules enacted on municipal transport financing for special programmes pur-suant to paragraph (1) of section 6 of the Municipal Transport Infrastructure Financing Act, as well as the other rules enacted by the Act of 20 December 2001 governing the Federal Financing of Seaports in Bremen, Hamburg, Mecklenburg-Western Pomerania, Lower Saxony and Schleswig-Holstein un-der paragraph (4) of Article 104a of the Basic Law as it stood up to 1 Septem-ber 2006 shall continue in force until their repeal. Amendment of the Municipal Transport Infrastructure Financing Act shall be permissible. The fourth sentence of paragraph (2) of Article 104b shall apply, *mutatis mutandis*. The other rules enacted in accordance with paragraph (4) of Article 104a of the Basic Law as it stood up to 1 September 2006 shall continue in force until 31 December 2019, provided no earlier repeal has been or is determined.

(3) The fifth sentence of paragraph (2) of Article 104b shall apply for the first time to regulations that enter into force after 31 December 2019.

Article 126 [Determination about continued applicability of law as federal law]

Disagreements concerning the continued applicability of law as federal law shall be resolved by the Federal Constitutional Court.

Article 127 [Extension of law to the French zone and to Berlin]

Within one year after promulgation of this Basic Law the Federal Government, with the consent of the governments of the *Länder* concerned, may extend to the *Länder* of Baden, Greater Berlin, Rhineland-Palatinate and Württemberg-Hohenzollern any law of the Administration of the Combined Economic Area, insofar as it remains in force as federal law under Article 124 or 125.

Article 128 [Continued authority to issue instructions]

Insofar as law that remains in force grants authority to issue instructions within the meaning of paragraph (5) of Article 84, this authority shall remain in existence until a law otherwise provides.

Article 129 [Continued authority to issue legal acts]

(1) Insofar as legal provisions that remain in force as federal law grant authority to issue statutory instruments or general administrative rules or to make administrative decisions in individual cases, such powers shall pass to the authorities that henceforth have competence over the subject matter. In cases of doubt the Federal Government shall decide in agreement with the Bundes-rat; such decisions shall be published.

(2) Insofar as legal provisions that remain in force as *Land* law grant such authority, it shall be exercised by the authorities competent under *Land* law.

(3) Insofar as legal provisions within the meaning of paragraphs (1) and (2) of this Article grant authority to amend or supplement the provisions themselves or to issue legal provisions that have the force of laws, such authority shall be deemed to have expired.

(4) The provisions of paragraphs (1) and (2) of this Article shall apply, *mutatis mutandis*,to legal provisions that refer to provisions no longer in force or to institutions no longer in existence.

Article 130 [Transfer of existing administrative institutions]

(1) Administrative agencies and other institutions that serve the public admi-nistration or the administration of justice and are not based on *Land* law or on agreements between *Länder*, as well as the Administrative Union of South West German Railways and the Administrative Council for Postal and Tele-communications Services for the French Occupation Zone, shall be placed under the control of the Federal Government. The Federal Government, with the consent of the Bundesrat, shall provide for their transfer, dissolution or liquidation.

(2) The supreme disciplinary authority for the personnel of these administra-tive bodies and institutions shall be the competent Federal Minister.

(3) Corporations and institutions under public law not directly subordinate to a *Land* nor based on agreements between *Länder* shall be under the super-vision of the competent highest federal authority.

Article 131 [Persons formerly in the public service]

The legal relations of persons, including refugees and expellees, who on 8 May 1945 were employed in the public service, have left the service for reasons other than those recognised by civil service regulations or collective bargaining agreements and have not yet been reinstated or are employed in positions that do not correspond to those they previously held shall be regulated by a federal law. The same shall apply, *mutatis mutandis*, to persons, including refugees and expellees, who on 8 May 1945 were entitled to pensions and related benefits and who for reasons other than those recognised by civil service regulations or collective bargaining agreements no longer receive any such pension or related benefits. Until the pertinent federal law takes effect, no legal claims may be made, unless *Land* law otherwise provides.

Article 132 [Retirement of civil servants]

(1) Civil servants and judges who enjoy life tenure when this Basic Law takes effect may, within six months after the Bundestag first convenes, be retired, suspended or transferred to lower-salaried positions if they lack the personal or professional aptitude for their present positions. This provision shall apply, *mutatis mutandis*, to salaried public employees other than civil servants or judges whose employment cannot be terminated at will. In the case of salaried employees whose employment may be terminated at will, notice periods longer than those set by collective bargaining agreements may be rescinded within the same period.

(2) The preceding provision shall not apply to members of the public service who are unaffected by the provisions regarding "Liberation from National Socialism and Militarism" or who are recognised victims of National Socialism, save on important personal grounds.

(3) Persons affected may have recourse to the courts in accordance with paragraph (4) of Article 19.

(4) Details shall be specified by a statutory instrument issued by the Federal Government with the consent of the Bundesrat.

Article 133 [Succession to the Administration of the Combined Economic Area]

The Federation shall succeed to the rights and duties of the Administration of the Combined Economic Area.

Article 134 [Succession to Reich assets]

(1) Reich assets shall, in principle, become federal assets.

(2) Insofar as such assets were originally intended to be used principally for administrative tasks not entrusted to the Federation under this Basic Law, they shall be transferred without compensation to the authorities now entrusted with such tasks, and to the extent that such assets are now being used, not merely temporarily, for administrative tasks that under this Basic Law are now performed by the *Länder*, they shall be transferred to the *Länder*. The Federation may also transfer other assets to the *Länder*.

(3) Assets that were placed at the disposal of the Reich without compensation by *Länder* or municipalities (associations of municipalities) shall revert to those *Länder* or municipalities (associations of municipalities) insofar as the Federation does not require them for its own administrative purposes.

(4) Details shall be regulated by a federal law requiring the consent of the Bundesrat.

Article 135 [Assets in case of territorial changes between the *Länder*]

(1) If, after 8 May 1945 and before the effective date of this Basic Law, an area has passed from one *Land* to another, the *Land* to which the area now belongs shall be entitled to the assets of the *Land* to which it previously belonged that are located in that area.

(2) The assets of *Länder* or of other corporations or institutions established under public law that no longer exist, insofar as they were originally intended to be used principally for administrative tasks or are now being so used, not

merely temporarily, shall pass to the *Land*, corporation or institution that now performs those tasks.

(3) Real property of *Länder* that no longer exist, including appurtenances, shall pass to the *Land* within which it is located, insofar as it is not among the assets already referred to in paragraph (1) of this Article.

(4) Insofar as an overriding interest of the Federation or the particular interest of a region requires, a federal law may depart from the rules prescribed by paragraphs (1) to (3) of this Article.

(5) In all other respects, the succession to and disposition of assets, insofar as it has not been effected before 1 January 1952 by agreement between the affected *Länder* or corporations or institutions established under public law, shall be regulated by a federal law requiring the consent of the Bundesrat.

(6) Holdings of the former *Land* of Prussia in enterprises established under private law shall pass to the Federation. Details shall be regulated by a federal law, which may also depart from this provision.

(7) Insofar as assets that, on the effective date of this Basic Law, would devolve upon a *Land* or a corporation or institution established under public law pursuant to paragraphs (1) to (3) of this Article have been disposed of by or pursuant to a *Land* law or in any other manner by the party thus entitled, the transfer of assets shall be deemed to have taken place before such disposition.

Article 135a [Old debts]

(1) Federal legislation enacted pursuant to paragraph (4) of Article 134 or paragraph (5) of Article 135 may also provide that the following debts shall not be discharged, or that they shall be discharged only in part:

1. debts of the Reich, of the former *Land* of Prussia, or of such other corporations and institutions established under public law as no longer exist;

2. such debts of the Federation or of corporations and institutions established under public law as are connected with the transfer of assets pursuant to

Article 89, 90, 134 or 135 and such debts of these bodies as arise from measures taken by the bodies designated in item 1;

3. such debts of the *Länder* or municipalities (associations of municipalities) as have arisen from measures taken by them before 1 August 1945 within the framework of administrative functions incumbent upon or delegated by the Reich to comply with orders of the occupying powers or to terminate a state of emergency resulting from the war.

(2) Paragraph (1) of this Article shall apply, *mutatis mutandis*, to debts of the German Democratic Republic or its institutions as well as to debts of the Federation or other corporations and institutions established under public law that are connected with the transfer of assets of the German Democratic Republic to the Federation, *Länder* or municipalities, and to debts arising from measures taken by the German Democratic Republic or its institutions.

Article 136 [First convening of the Bundesrat]

(1) The Bundesrat shall convene for the first time on the day on which the Bundestag first convenes.

(2) Until the election of the first Federal President, his powers shall be exercised by the President of the Bundesrat. He shall not have authority to dissolve the Bundestag.

Article 137 [Right of state employees to stand for election]

(1) The right of civil servants, other salaried public employees, professional or volunteer members of the Armed Forces and judges to stand for election in the Federation, in the *Länder* or in the municipalities may be restricted by a law.

(2) The election of the first Bundestag, of the first Federal Convention and of the first Federal President shall be governed by an electoral law to be enacted by the Parliamentary Council.

(3) Until the Federal Constitutional Court is established, its authority under paragraph (2) of Article 41 shall be exercised by the German High Court for the Combined Economic Area, which shall make determinations in accordance with its procedural rules.

Article 138 [South German notaries]

Changes in the rules governing the notarial profession as it now exists in the *Länder* of Baden, Bavaria, Württemberg-Baden and Württemberg-Hohenzollern shall require the consent of the governments of these *Länder*.

Article 139 [Continued applicability of denazification provisions]

The legal provisions enacted for the "Liberation of the German People from National Socialism and Militarism" shall not be affected by the provisions of this Basic Law.

Article 140 [Law of religious denominations]

The provisions of Articles 136, 137, 138, 139 and 141 of the German Constitution of 11 August 1919 shall be an integral part of this Basic Law.

Article 141 ["Bremen Clause"]

The first sentence of paragraph (3) of Article 7 shall not apply in any *Land* in which *Land* law otherwise provided on 1 January 1949.

Article 142 [Reservation in favour of basic rights in *Land* constitutions]

Notwithstanding Article 31, provisions of *Land* constitutions shall also remain in force insofar as they guarantee basic rights in conformity with Articles 1 to 18 of this Basic Law.

Article 142a (repealed)

Article 143 [Duration of derogations from the Basic Law]

(1) The law in the territory specified in Article 3 of the Unification Treaty may derogate from provisions of this Basic Law for a period extending no later than 31 December 1992 insofar and so long as disparate circumstances make full compliance impossible. Derogations may not violate paragraph (2) of Article 19 and must be compatible with the principles specified in paragraph (3) of Article 79.

(2) Derogations from Titles II, VIII, VIIIa, IX, X and XI shall be permissible for a period extending to no later than 31 December 1995.

(3) Independently of paragraphs (1) and (2) of this Article, Article 41 of the Unification Treaty and the rules for its implementation shall also remain in effect insofar as they provide for the irreversibility of acts interfering with property rights in the territory specified in Article 3 of this Treaty.

Article 143a [Exclusive legislative power concerning federal railways]

(1) The Federation shall have exclusive power to legislate with respect to all matters arising from the transformation of federal railways administered by the Federation into business enterprises. Paragraph (5) of Article 87e shall apply, *mutatis mutandis*. Civil servants employed by federal railways may be assigned by a law to render services to federal railways established under private law without prejudice to their legal status or the responsibility of their employer.

(2) Laws enacted pursuant to paragraph (1) of this Article shall be executed by the Federation.

(3) The Federation shall continue to be responsible for local passenger services of the former federal railways until 31 December 1995. The same shall apply to the corresponding functions of rail transport administration. Details shall be regulated by a federal law requiring the consent of the Bundesrat.

Article 143b [Transformation of the Deutsche Bundespost]

(1) The special trust Deutsche Bundespost shall be transformed into enterprises under private law in accordance with a federal law. The Federation shall have exclusive power to legislate with respect to all matters arising from this transformation.

(2) The exclusive rights of the Federation existing before the transformation may be transferred by a federal law for a transitional period to the enterprises that succeed to the Deutsche Bundespost Postdienst and to the Deutsche Bundespost Telekom. The Federation may not surrender its majority interest in the enterprise that succeeds to the Deutsche Bundespost Postdienst until at least five years after the law takes effect. To do so shall require a federal law with the consent of the Bundesrat.

(3) Federal civil servants employed by the Deutsche Bundespost shall be given positions in the private enterprises that succeed to it, without prejudice to their legal status or the responsibility of their employer. The enterprises shall exercise the employer's authority. Details shall be regulated by a federal law.

Article 143c [Compensation for the cessation of joint tasks]

(1) From 1 January 2007 until 31 December 2019, the *Länder* shall be entitled to receive annual payments from the federal budget as compensation for losing the Federation's financial contributions resulting from the abolition of the joint tasks of extension and construction of institutions of higher education, including university hospitals and educational planning, as well as for losing financial assistance for the improvement of municipal traffic infrastructure and for the promotion of social housing. Until 31 December 2013, these amounts are to be determined by averaging the financial share of the Federation for the years 2000 to 2008.

(2) Until 31 December 2013, the payments pursuant to paragraph (1) shall be distributed among the *Länder* in the form of:

1. fixed annual payments the amounts of which shall be determined according to the average share of each *Land* during the period 2000 to 2003;

2. payments earmarked for the functional area of the former joint financing.

(3) Until the end of 2013, the Federation and the *Länder* shall review the extent to which the financing allotted to individual *Länder* pursuant to paragraph (1) is still appropriate and necessary for the discharge of their tasks. Beginning on 1 January 2014, the earmarking pursuant to item 2 of paragraph (2) of the financial means allotted under paragraph (1) shall cease; the earmarking for the volume of the means for investment purposes shall remain unchanged. Agreements resulting from Solidarity Pact II shall remain unaffected.

(4) Details shall be regulated by a federal law which shall require the consent of the Bundesrat.

Article 143d [Transitional provisions relating to consolidation assistance]

(1) Articles 109 and 115 in the version in force until 31 July 2009 shall apply for the last time to the 2010 budget. Articles 109 and 115 in the version in force as from 1 August 2009 shall apply for the first time to the 2011 budget; debit authorisations existing on 31 December 2010 for special trusts already established shall remain unaffected. In the period from 1 January 2011 to 31 December 2019, the *Länder* may, in accordance with their applicable legal regulations, derogate from the provisions of paragraph (3) of Article 109. The budgets of the *Länder* are to be planned in such a way that the 2020 budget fulfils the requirements of the fifth sentence of paragraph (3) of Article 109. In the period from 1 January 2011 to 31 December 2015, the Federation may derogate from the provisions of the second sentence of paragraph (2) of Article 115. The reduction of the existing deficits should begin with the 2011 budget. The annual budgets are to be planned in such a way that the 2016 budget satisfies the requirement of the second sentence of paragraph (2) of Article 115; details shall be regulated by federal law.

(2) As assistance for compliance with the provisions of paragraph (3) of Article 109 after 1 January 2020, the *Länder* of Berlin, Bremen, Saarland, Saxony-Anhalt and Schleswig-Holstein may receive, for the period 2011 to 2019, consolidation assistance from the federal budget in the global amount of 800 million euros annually. The respective amounts are 300 million euros for Bremen, 260 million euros for Saarland and 80 million euros each for Berlin, Saxony-Anhalt, and Schleswig-Holstein. The assistance payments shall be allocated on the basis of an administrative agreement under the terms of a federal law requiring the consent of the Bundesrat. These grants require a complete reduction of financial deficits by the end of 2020. The details, especially the annual steps to be taken to reduce financial deficits and the supervision of the reduction of financial deficits by the Stability Council, along with the consequences entailed in case of failure to carry out the step-by-step reduction, shall be regulated by a federal law requiring the consent of the Bundesrat and by an administrative agreement. Consolidation assistance shall not be granted concurrently with redevelopment assistance awarded on the grounds of an extreme budgetary emergency.

(3) The financial burden resulting from the granting of the consolidation assistance shall be borne equally by the Federation and the *Länder*, to be financed from their share of revenue from the turnover tax. Details shall be regulated by a federal law requiring the consent of the Bundesrat.

(4) As assistance for future autonomous compliance with the provisions of paragraph (3) of Article 109, the *Länder* of Bremen and Saarland may receive redevelopment assistance from the federal budget in the global amount of 800 million euros annually from 1 January 2020. To this end, the *Länder* shall adopt measures to reduce excessive debts and to strengthen their economic and financial capacity. Details shall be regulated by a federal law requiring the consent of the Bundesrat. This redevelopment assistance shall not be granted concurrently with redevelopment assistance awarded on the grounds of an extreme budgetary emergency.

Article 143e [Federal motorways, transformation of commissioned administration]

(1) Notwithstanding the provisions of paragraph (2) of Article 90, the federal motorways shall be administered on federal commission by the *Länder* or such self-governing bodies as are competent under *Land* law until no later than 31 December 2020. The Federation shall regulate the transformation from commissioned administration to federal administration under paragraphs (2) and (4) of Article 90 by means of a federal law requiring the consent of the Bundesrat.

(2) At the request of a *Land*, to be made by 31 December 2018, the Federation, notwithstanding the provisions of paragraph (2) of Article 90, shall assume administrative responsibility for the other federal trunk roads, insofar as they lie within the territory of that *Land*, with effect from 1 January 2021.

(3) By a federal law with the consent of the Bundesrat, it may be regulated that a *Land*, upon application, takes over, on commission of the Federation, the function of administering plan approval and planning permission for the construction and alteration of federal motorways and other federal trunk roads for which the Federation has assumed administrative responsibility under paragraph (4) of Article 90 or paragraph (2) of Article 143e and on what conditions this function may be transferred back.

Article 143f [Financial relations within the federal system of government]

Article 143d, the Act regulating Revenue Sharing between the Federation and the *Länder* (Financial Equalisation Act) and other laws enacted on the basis of paragraph (2) of Article 107 as it stands from 1 January 2020 shall expire if, after 31 December 2030, the Federal Government, the Bundestag or at least three *Länder* acting jointly have requested negotiations on a restructuring of financial relations within the federal system of government and, when five years have elapsed since the Federal President was notified of the negotiation request made by the Federal Government, the Bundestag or the *Länder*, no statutory restructuring of financial relations within the federal system of government has entered into force. The expiry date shall be published in the Federal Law Gazette.

Article 143g [Continued applicability of Article 107]

For the regulation of the distribution of tax revenue, of financial equalisation between *Länder* and of federal supplementary grants, Article 107 as it stood until the entry into force of the Basic Law Amendment Act of 13 July 2017 shall continue to be applied until 31 December 2019.

Article 144 [Ratification of the Basic Law – Berlin]

(1) This Basic Law shall require ratification by the parliaments of two thirds of the German *Länder* in which it is initially to apply.

(2) Insofar as the application of this Basic Law is subject to restrictions in any *Land* listed in Article 23 or in any part thereof, such *Land* or part thereof shall have the right to send representatives to the Bundestag in accordance with Article 38 and to the Bundesrat in accordance with Article 50.

Article 145 [Entry into force of the Basic Law]

(1) The Parliamentary Council, with the participation of the members for Greater Berlin, shall confirm the ratification of this Basic Law in public session and shall certify and promulgate it.

(2) This Basic Law shall take effect at the end of the day on which it is promulgated.

(3) It shall be published in the Federal Law Gazette.

Article 146 [Duration of the Basic Law]

This Basic Law, which, since the achievement of the unity and freedom of Germany, applies to the entire German people, shall cease to apply on the day on which a constitution freely adopted by the German people takes effect.

Extracts from the German Constitution of 11 August 1919 (Weimar Constitution)

Religion and Religious Societies

Article 136

(1) Civil and political rights and duties shall be neither dependent upon nor restricted by the exercise of religious freedom.

(2) Enjoyment of civil and political rights and eligibility for public office shall be independent of religious affiliation.

(3) No person shall be required to disclose his religious convictions. The authorities shall have the right to inquire into a person's membership of a religious society only to the extent that rights or duties depend upon it or that a statistical survey mandated by a law so requires.

(4) No person may be compelled to perform any religious act or ceremony, to participate in religious exercises or to take a religious form of oath.

Article 137

(1) There shall be no state church.

(2) The freedom to form religious societies shall be guaranteed. The union of religious societies within the territory of the Reich shall be subject to no restrictions.

(3) Religious societies shall regulate and administer their affairs independently within the limits of the law that applies to all. They shall confer their offices without the participation of the state or the civil community.

(4) Religious societies shall acquire legal capacity according to the general provisions of civil law.

(5) Religious societies shall remain corporations under public law insofar as they have enjoyed that status in the past. Other religious societies shall be granted the same rights upon application, if their constitution and the number of their members give assurance of their permanency. If two or more religious societies established under public law unite into a single organisation, it too shall be a corporation under public law.

(6) Religious societies that are corporations under public law shall be entitled to levy taxes on the basis of the civil taxation lists in accordance with *Land* law.

(7) Associations whose purpose is to foster a philosophical creed shall have the same status as religious societies.

(8) Such further regulation as may be required for the implementation of these provisions shall be a matter for *Land* legislation.

Article 138

(1) Rights of religious societies to public subsidies on the basis of a law, contract or special grant shall be redeemed by legislation of the *Länder*. The principles governing such redemption shall be established by the Reich.

(2) Property rights and other rights of religious societies or associations in their institutions, foundations and other assets intended for purposes of worship, education or charity shall be guaranteed.

Article 139

Sunday and holidays recognised by the state shall remain protected by law as days of rest from work and of spiritual improvement.

Article 141

To the extent that a need exists for religious services and pastoral work in the army, in hospitals, in prisons or in other public institutions, religious societies shall be permitted to provide them, but without compulsion of any kind.

Visit

www.highcontentbooks.com

Printed in Great Britain
by Amazon